YOUR FAITHFUL SERVANT

Bronze replica of the statue of Blake by FW Pomeroy which stands on the Cornhill in Bridgwater. Unveiled on 4th October, 1900, to this day it is the only statue of Robert Blake in a public place. [*Admiral Blake Museum*

YOUR FAITHFUL SERVANT

Insights into the life of the Cromwellian Navy
from the letters, despatches and orders of
Robert Blake, General at Sea

Admiral Blake Museum, Bridgwater

PRYOR PUBLICATIONS
WHITSTABLE AND WALSALL

PRYOR PUBLICATIONS
WHITSTABLE AND WALSALL

Specialist in Facsimile Reproductions.

MEMBER OF
INDEPENDENT PUBLISHERS GUILD

75 Dargate Road, Yorkletts, Whitstable,
Kent CT5 3AE, England.
Tel. & Fax: (01227) 274655

Email: alan@pryor-publish.clara.net

http://home.clara.net/pryor-publish

Kent Exporter of the Year Awards Winner 1998

ISBN 0 94601487-6

©Blake Museum May 2000

A full list of Titles sent free on request.

Printed by
Hillman Printers
(Frome) Ltd
Handlemaker Road,
Marston Trading Estate,
Frome, Somerset BA11 4RW.
Tel: 01373 473526   Fax: 01373 451852

CONTENTS

ILLUSTRATIONS

Front cover illustration
Engraving of Admiral Blake by Rarenet. Like a number of other likenesses, it seems to have been based on the contemporary portrait of Blake by an unknown artist, which hangs in the National Maritime Museum. [Admiral Blake Museum]

FOREWORD

This book was produced to commemorate the four hundredth anniversary of the birth of Robert Blake, England's forgotten admiral. It is not intended as a detailed expose of the Navy of the English Republic[1], nor is it a detailed or definitive account of Blake's life and achievements[2], nor is it a comprehensive edition of his letters[3]. Other fuller accounts, to which we are heavily indebted, are readily available. It is simply an attempt to highlight aspects of a little known but very important period in the development of the British Navy as they appear in the letters of one of its most important architects - Robert Blake.

It was the late Dr. J.R. Powell, a prolific Blake scholar and lifelong friend of Bridgwater and the Admiral Blake Museum, who provided the inspiration for this book. One day in the spring of 1997, whilst sorting though a mass of unclassified Museum ephemera, we came across a sheaf of old typewritten transcripts of over 200 of the letters of Robert Blake. Subsequent investigation suggested that this had formed part of the research that Powell had done in preparation for his major work more than sixty years ago. Once we began to read the letters it became clear that the most fitting memorial to Blake for his four hundredth anniversary was to bring his letters to public attention once more.

We try to let Blake and his colleagues tell their own story through selected extracts from letters which were primarily concerned with getting things done - they did not have the time or inclination to engage in much social, philosophical or personal discourse. Nevertheless, as we read them, we joined Blake, who was almost constantly at sea during eight

---

[1]   Bernard Capp : Cromwell's Navy - The Fleet and the English Revolution 1648-1660 (Clarendon Paperbacks, O.U.P. 1988);

[2]   There are several excellent biographies of Blake, including that of J.R.Powell. The most up-to-date scholarly account is Michael Baumber : General-at-Sea - Robert Blake and the Seventeenth Century Revolution in Naval Warfare (John Murray, 1989);

[3]   J.R. Powell : Letters of Robert Blake (Navy Records Society, 1937).

years of what must have been one of the busiest and most exciting periods in the history of the British Navy. We invite you to do the same.

We hope this book will be of particular interest to anyone who has a fascination for the Navy, with the Seventeenth Century and the English Revolution, or who simply wishes to listen directly to the voices of the past.

This has been a work of collaboration of Museum Staff and volunteers. Particular thanks go to Sarah Harbige, Museums Officer, who proofed the manuscript and offered many positive suggestions; to Paul Wiggins, who started it all; to Ingrid Wiggins who re-typed the transcripts; to Jack Gillespie who photographed the exhibits and to Mary Thyne, our former Hon. Curator, whose knowledge and enthusiasm has been a constant source of inspiration.

THE ORIGINAL LETTERS AND PAPERS

The most comprehensive readily available printed source for these is Powell's work (see above) which we have used freely in making this selection - those extracts to be found in this source are marked with an asterisk (*). The original documents are to be found in a number of public and private collections which we have attempted to identify:

Add. MSS	Additional Manuscripts Collection in the British Library
Portland MSS	Manuscripts of the Duke of Portland at Welbeck Abbey
Rawlinson A	Rawlinson MSS in the Bodleian Library, Oxford
S.P.	State Papers, Domestic, Interregnum in the Public Record Office
Tanner MSS	Tanner Manuscripts in the Bodleian Library, Oxford
Thurloe	Letters and papers of John Thurloe T. Birch (ed.)

Blake dictated his letters to a number of different clerks. Since there were no standard conventions at the time, spelling and punctuation differ considerably from one letter to another. For the ease of the modern reader, the letters have been rendered in standard modern spelling and punctuation. The original grammar and syntax has not been altered; nor has the sometimes idiosyncratic use of capital letters.

NOTE ON DATES

Until 1752 England used the **Julian** calendar, whereas most countries in Europe had converted to the **Gregorian** calendar by the middle of the Seventeenth Century. The **Julian** dates are always given in this book, as they were those used in England at the time. Additionally the **legal** New Year began on 25th March following the beginning of the historical year and contemporary documents may use either or both dates. For simplicity the historical year (i.e. beginning 1st January) is used in this book.

D.J. Sebborn

> "As he lived, so he continued to the death, faithful."
> Captain Henry Hatsell, the Naval Agent in Plymouth,
> on the death of Blake

CHAPTER 1 WHO WAS ROBERT BLAKE?

Mention the British Navy and everyone's heard of Drake and Nelson - but Blake? Yet in his lifetime Robert Blake was a national hero, first as a soldier in the Civil War and then as a naval commander. When he died he was given a prestigious state funeral.

Amongst the first English admirals to keep a fleet at sea through the winter, he developed the techniques of blockade and amphibious landing. Twice he destroyed fleets in harbour under the guns of shore forts. Later admirals were to copy this - Nelson wrote, "I shall never be the equal of Blake." Yet his contribution and that of his colleagues to the daily routine and working of the British Navy was equally as important. In everything he maintained humility, humanity and a total dedication to duty. He is the unsung midwife of the British Navy and deserves to rank with Drake and Nelson.

This was an achievement in itself. But it is even more notable when you remember that he was only appointed to naval command, with, as far as we know limited experience of the sea, at the age of fifty and remained almost constantly at sea for the last eight years of his life.

EARLY LIFE

Robert Blake, born in 1598, was the eldest child of the large family of a well-to-do Bridgwater merchant - both his father and grandfather had been mayors of Bridgwater, and two of his younger brothers were later to fill that office. A restless man, who loved Bridgwater but could never settle in it, Blake spent most of his life away from his hometown. Recommended by the master of the Bridgwater Free Grammar School, he spent years at St. Alban's Hall and Wadham College, Oxford, where he tried and failed to establish himself as an academic.

He returned to Bridgwater to sort out his family's affairs about the time of his father's death in 1625, for he is recorded as living in the town in 1628.

For about ten years he disappeared from Bridgwater and Somerset. Possibly he tried to establish a business in Dorchester - a merchant named Robert Blake was active in that town around 1629-30. At some stage in the early part of his life he may have lived at Schiedam in Holland, perhaps to act as overseas agent for the family business. In 1638 he was back in Bridgwater, around the time his mother died.

In April 1640 King Charles I called his first Parliament for eleven years and Robert Blake was elected as one of the Members for Bridgwater. We can only surmise from his later career and views that he was one of many MPs committed to curtailing the power of the King; certainly his brother Humphrey was already known for his Puritan views. However, the King soon dissolved the Short Parliament before Robert could make his mark, if indeed he ever attended. He was not re-elected to the Parliament called in November 1640, supplanted by another candidate of higher social status. Up until 1642 Robert Blake's career had been a series of false starts. With the outbreak of the Civil War, Blake found his vocation.

BLAKE THE SOLDIER

Blake joined the Parliamentary Army of Sir John Horner and became a Captain in Alexander Popham's regiment. At the defence of Bristol in 1643 he earned a reputation as a determined and doughty fighter. He fought on after Fiennes had surrendered the city and Prince Rupert, the Royalist commander was minded to hang him. He reappeared again defending Lyme against Prince Maurice. A subordinate officer at the start of the siege he seems to have been in command by the end. A stubborn defence and the support of Warwick's parliamentary navy in the Bay saw off the Royalists.

Blake moved on to Taunton where in 1644 he was raising a new regiment. Left behind as Governor with a makeshift force of 1000, he endured three sieges between October 1644 and July 1645, successively blockaded by Edmund Wyndham, Governor of Bridgwater, Sir John Berkley and Lord Goring. By the end of his heroic defence of Taunton, the town, with the

Plate I Blake's birthplace in Bridgwater
Situated next to the old Town Mill and the River Parrett, the building has housed
the Admiral Blake Museum since 1926. The house was built in the late 15th
Century and survived the partial destruction of the town in 1645 by Fairfax and
the New Model Army. Blake's father's will left the house jointly to his two oldest
sons, Robert and Humphrey, but it is likely that, with Robert so frequently away
from Bridgwater, it was the centre of the family shipping business, run by
Humphrey. The Commonwealth flag flies from the flagpole.

[Admiral Blake Museum]

3

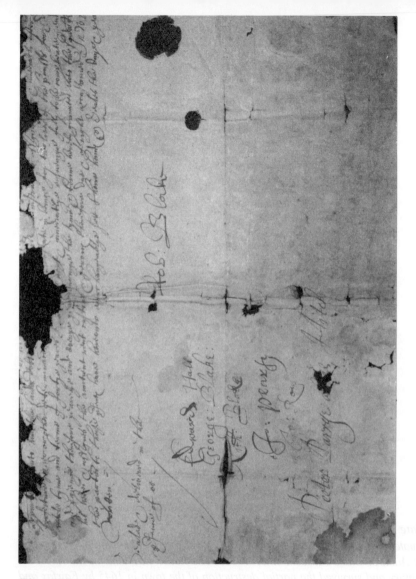

Plate II Fragment of a land transaction

This deed dated April 1649 transferred lands and rights in Robert Blake's manor of Crandon cum Puriton to Robert Bowditch. It may represent a stage at which Robert was simplifying his affairs in Bridgwater prior to going to sea as commander of the English Navy. It bears the Blake family seal, and, in addition to Robert, is signed by two other members of the family. [Admiral Blake Museum]

4

exception of the castle, was all but destroyed and the people starving - but the news had made Blake a hero in London. In November 1645 Blake went on to besiege and capture the last Royalist stronghold in Somerset, Dunster Castle, which surrendered in April 1646.

By the end of the First Civil War Blake was an established figure in the new hierarchy. Governor of Taunton, again MP for Bridgwater, his name appears in both Parliamentary and County Committees. Staunchly anti-royalist, he was nevertheless a man of conservative social and religious views - typical of the Presbyterian establishment of the time. The growing differences between the army and parliament were undoubtedly an embarrassment to him. Significantly he took no part in the trial and execution of the King in January 1649.

GENERAL AT SEA

Unexpectedly Blake was appointed one of three Generals-at-Sea in February 1649. His two colleagues were also men of the South West. Edward Popham, a close friend was from an important landed Somerset family. Richard Deane, a Devon man, was the commander of the artillery in the New Model Army. To appoint landsmen to naval commands quite usual at the time. Only Popham had previous naval experience. More significantly the three were **army** officers and were to share command.

At this point the Navy was regarded as unreliable, even disloyal. The year before some ships had deserted to the Royalists. Warwick, the Parliamentary commander, had a reputation of inaction. What was needed were leaders who were men of action and proven administrators; above all men who could be trusted by both Parliament and the army.

THE PURSUIT OF THE ROYALISTS

Blake and Deane spent their first weeks in office issuing orders to make the Navy a reliable fighting unit again[1]. Then they were off to deal with Rupert's royalist squadron, which they shut up, in Kinsale in southern Ireland. Only one of the three Generals-at-Sea could be spared to

---

[1] See 2.2, 2.12, 2.13, 3.3, 4.4, 4.7, 4.10, 4.13, 4.14, 6.2, 6.3.

continue the blockade - two were needed for important administrative tasks in connection with the reconquest of Ireland. Blake, chosen by lot, stayed out into his first rough winter at sea. He seems to have taken to his new life, and turned down the offer of a very senior military command in Ireland (**8.1**). Twice bad weather drove Blake's squadron from Kinsale and on the second occasion, in October 1649, Rupert escaped and headed for Portugal.

In March 1650 Blake sailed to deal with Rupert. The latter had sought safety in the Tagus, where King John of Portugal was sympathetic to the royalist cause. On arriving Blake attempted to force his way in, only to be fired at by the forts defending Lisbon. He retired to blockade the entrance to the river. To mount a full scale attack on Rupert in harbour would precipitate war with Portugal so Blake had to content himself with prolonged diplomatic negotiations to persuade King John to force Rupert out to sea.

Rupert made a first bid for freedom only to be forced back by Blake (**7.1**). In September Rupert made a second attempt to break out and there was a direct confrontation between the ships of the opposing admirals (**7.2**). Again Rupert retreated behind the safety of the Portuguese forts. A week later Blake's ships were able to attack and capture a number of the incoming Portuguese Brazil fleet. Shortage of supplies and water forced Blake to abandon the blockade of the Tagus and sail south to Cadiz. Here he encountered a potentially hostile French squadron. His capture of one of them has passed into Blake folklore (**7.3**).

Meanwhile Rupert took the opportunity to slip out of the Tagus and head for the Mediterranean, thinking Blake had gone home. As soon as Blake heard the news he gave chase. In early November part of Rupert's fleet was forced into Cartagena. Blake was not to be frustrated as he had been at Lisbon and wrote directly to the King of Spain. Apparently believing they would be handed over by the Spanish authorities, the royalist ships made a dash for freedom. The attempt was botched and the royalist ships were wrecked. Rupert sought the safety of a French port. Though Blake

6

never brought Rupert to book, a cause of great disappointment to him (**2.2**), the royalist admiral was no longer a serious threat.

A few royalist strongholds remained. In 1651 Blake led an expedition to the Scilly Isles, a centre of royalist privateering against English and Dutch vessels. It was decided that Blake should take the Scilly Isles before the Dutch did. Blake ordered an attack on the island of Tresco. At the second attempt it was stormed in a difficult amphibious landing. A month later the Royalist commander, Sir John Grenville, surrendered on generous terms.

Blake now mounted an expedition against Jersey. The royalists held strong positions and the wind and current proved difficult. In worsening weather and fading light Blake sent the boats ashore in a combined operation led by seamen. The royalist positions crumbled and it was only a matter of time before the commander Sir George Carteret surrendered (**7.4**).

THE DUTCH WAR

England's simmering quarrel with the Dutch boiled over into war in May 1652 when Blake's fleet clashed with that of Tromp off Dover (**7.5**). The Anglo-Dutch War was Blake's real baptism of fire. He and the other inexperienced English commanders faced Dutch admirals - Martin Harpertzoon Tromp, Michiel de Ruyter, Witte Corneliszoon de With - more experienced and skilful than they. The Dutch could not afford to give way, so dependent was their country on overseas trade. Control of the English Channel was hotly contested.

The scale of the fighting was greater than that with the Spanish Armada. Hundreds of ships were involved and there were terrible casualties. In numbers the fleets were evenly matched. The Dutch ships were more manoeuvrable but carried lighter firepower, usually mounting brass guns, as did other European navies at the time (**7.3**). The English ships drew more water and mounted heavier iron cannon. In the treacherous inland shoals of the Narrow Seas the Dutch had the advantage, but where an English ship could close with one or more Dutch vessels in deep water, the English ship always carried the day.

Blake was sent to intercept the Dutch merchant fleet from the East Indies off the Shetland Islands. Bad weather struck. Blake kept his fleet intact but the Dutch were scattered to the winds. Briefly the Dutch commander Tromp was in disgrace, and command passed to the brave but unpopular de With.

Meanwhile the Dutch Admiral de Ruyter had been sent down the English Channel to accompany the incoming West Indies fleet. In September, having got the better of Ayscue's squadron and given Penn's squadron the slip, de Ruyter neared home. De With brought his fleet out to escort him.

Blake's fleet met that of de With and de Ruyter on 28th September. More by luck than judgement the English ships managed to get amongst the Dutch, where their superior firepower did great execution. The Dutch retreated to the safety of their harbours. The Battle of the Kentish Knock revealed the strengths and the weaknesses of the English fleet in a large action. Vice Admiral Penn had run aground, Rear Admiral Bourne and Captain Badiley had been left dangerously exposed. Blake and the English admirals still had much to learn.

The spiralling cost of the war and the expansion of the fleet gave the government cause for concern. Some of those in power thought, now that the Dutch had been defeated, the war could be ended. The result was that Blake's fleet became much depleted. The seamen's loyalty was in doubt because they had not been paid. Those ships Blake had under his command in the Downs had not been refitted or re-supplied.

In November Tromp, now restored to command, put to sea to escort a merchant fleet down the English Channel. His warships outnumbered those of Blake by two to one. Blake's captains advised against engaging the Dutch. Blake ordered his fleet to shadow the Dutch fleet as it sailed southwards, but off Dungeness the two fleets clashed (**7.6**). Blake's own ship, the *Triumph* became detached from the main battle, and the ships at the rear of Blake's fleet failed to engage. Darkness brought the end to the action, but not before two English warships were lost. The Dutch got their merchant fleet away safely, and, in effect, now had control of the Narrow Seas.

The defeat of Dungeness brought bitter recriminations (**2.3**). Blake insisted on a court of enquiry and offered to resign. Six captains, including the General's own brother Benjamin, were disciplined. In the event Robert did not resign and four of the six captains were reinstated.
The real lessons of the Battles of the Kentish Knock and Dungeness were learned. New Fighting Instructions were drawn up. The scope for individual captains to interpret their orders began to be curtailed. The use of hired-armed merchant ships was discontinued, since these could not always be relied upon in the heat of action. A new disciplinary code, the Articles of War, was adopted. A new Admiralty Committee was appointed. At Blake's insistence, the pay of seamen was raised and prize money increased (**4.13**). Money was voted to reprovision the fleet.

In February 1653 Tromp began to escort the incoming Dutch merchant fleet up the English Channel. The English admirals were determined to prevent the Dutch making home port. However the squadrons of the Dutch fleet acting together found the English fleet scattered and sailed in to take advantage. Blake and Deane in the *Triumph* were hard pressed in the middle of the fighting, with Penn's squadron vainly trying to come to their aid. The prompt action of John Lawson, Blake's Vice Admiral of the Red, saved the day and justified the reorganisation of command after Dungeness.
Monck's squadron eventually arrived and, in deep water off Portland, the English fleet pounded the Dutch warships, whilst Monck's frigates chased the Dutch merchantmen. The battle continued for two days up the Channel as Tromp tried to bring his charges home, until eventually he was forced to seek safety amongst the shoals under Cape Griz Nez where the

English could not follow.

It was a victory, but not as complete as it might have been. The casualties on both sides were terrible (**2.4**). At least five Dutch ships were sunk, and one flag officer and twelve captains killed. A news sheet of the time gave a graphic description of the captured Dutch prizes that arrived in English ports:

"All the men-of-war who are taken are much dyed with blood, their masts and tackles being moiled with brains, hair, pieces of skulls; dreadful sights though glorious, as being a signal token of the lord's goodness to this Nation."

There was heavy loss of life on the English side too, particularly on the *Triumph*. Amongst the 80 casualties on this ship alone were its Captain and Blake's Secretary, both killed, and Blake himself, wounded in the thigh.

Infection set in and Blake was put ashore. Ignoring the advice of his doctors, he returned to work at the Admiralty. In June he gathered a makeshift squadron (**2.5**) to come to the aid of Monck at the Battle of the Gabbard. Blake's arrival had a considerable psychological effect - the sight of his flag raised a cheer in the English ships and convinced the Dutch to seek the safety of shallow water.

Blake's health broke. He was not expected to live and there was speculation about his successor. This time it took his body longer to recover and he was absent from the final conclusive victory over the Dutch at the Battle of Scheveningen in July 1653.

RETURN TO THE MEDITERRANEAN

In August 1654 the indispensable Blake was sent out to the Mediterranean. Opinion at home in the corridors of power was divided between those who wanted a confrontation with France for the consistent support that country had given the Royalists and those who favoured war

10

with Spain, the policy which had been traditional since Elizabethan times. In any event it was in England's interests to see the war between France and Spain prolonged, since while it continued neither was a threat to England.

Blake's precise orders are unclear. There was much secret correspondence between Cromwell and Blake, but we can only guess at its content. It seems that, while Penn was being sent with an expedition, the "Western Design", to attack Spain in the New World, Blake was to patrol the Straits and the Western Mediterranean to frustrate French actions against the Spanish in Naples. His second objective was to seize the Spanish treasure fleet. In a situation of undeclared war this required discretion. It is not surprising that Blake, the most experienced and trustworthy of England's admirals, was given the task.

The presence of Blake's fleet in the Straits prevented French reinforcements reaching their Mediterranean fleet and deterred the Portuguese from sending their fleet to help the French. On hearing of Blake's arrival in the Mediterranean, the French expedition to Naples retired to Toulon. Blake's first objective had been achieved.

Having intervened successfully in one foreign war Blake tried to intervene in a second. The Moslem Turks and Christian Venetians were at war in Crete. The Sultan had sent a squadron to Tunis to persuade its Moslem ruler to throw his fleet behind the attack on Crete. It was not difficult to find an excuse to attack any Moslem ruler in North Africa, for all had Christian slaves.

In April 1655, Blake used his own initiative to attack the Turkish squadron sheltering at Porto Farina (7.7). The larger ships engaged the shore forts while the frigates went inshore. Boarding parties soon swept away all opposition and all eight Turkish ships were burned. In a confined harbour, with an unfavourable wind the English ships got to open sea by the novel expedient of 'warping out', i.e. pulling on anchors dropped outside the harbour before entry.

11

Though the opposition had been feeble and English casualties light, it was a classic assault on a fleet in harbour. It was just as well that it had been an unequivocal victory; Blake was almost certainly exceeding his orders. In the event Cromwell was pleased. The victory speeded up the treaty with the neighbouring Moslem power of Algiers and the wholesale release of English, Irish and even Dutch prisoners (5.28) who had been held as slaves.

Blake, now free to pursue the Spaniards, set off for the Straits where a large Spanish fleet had put to sea. In August Blake sighted the Spanish fleet but did not attack. The swell was too high so that the lower gun ports could not be opened; his orders were not explicit. Were these Blake's excuses, or did Blake know that the Spaniards were not destined for the West Indies? Cromwell was furious. Blake was ordered to remain out to await and ambush the Spanish Plate fleet. He was in no condition so to do. His ships were "foul" i.e. encrusted with marine growth below the waterline, from being out too long in a warm sea, and therefore slow and unmanoeuvreable. With a shortage of food, water and other necessities, and the crews discontented, Blake took the decision to return home in September.

Blake did have some important successes to show, whilst Penn's expedition, which had returned the previous month had less. In the event Blake's show of strength against the French did spur the French to make a treaty with England.

BLAKE'S LAST VOYAGE

Blake had scarcely returned from his previous voyage when he was named to lead a new expedition against Spain. Blake asked for a colleague to share his responsibilities, and Cromwell appointed one of his close supporters, Edward Mountagu. The two men were very different. Mountagu, though much younger and of aristocratic birth, was eager to learn from the dour and ailing republican and quickly charmed his way into the old man's affections.

It was important to get the fleet to sea. There had been discontent in the Channel fleet. To draw the teeth of any mutiny money was voted to pay the seamen's arrears and Lawson, the perceived ringleader, was named Vice Admiral of Blake's expedition, to get him out of harm's way. However Lawson and three captains resigned rather than sail for Spain.

The fleet sailed in March 1656. An attack on Cadiz and the seizure of Gibraltar were contemplated, but abandoned. Soon the problems of supplying the fleet again became urgent. The English government succeeded in making a treaty with Portugal giving the English friendly ports from which to supply the fleet. Concluding the treaty was not without difficulties - there was an attack on the English representative in Lisbon and Blake and Mountagu waited with increasing impatience for the promised compensation for losses sustained as a result of Portuguese actions in 1650, when Blake had last visited Lisbon.

It became clear that there was to be no dynamic strike against Spain and a long blockade was in prospect. Frustrated, Cromwell ordered some of the ships home. The blockade tightened. Squadrons were sent to attack Vigo and Malaga. Finally in September part of a small incoming Spanish treasure fleet was intercepted by Stayner's squadron and captured.

Mountagu came home with the larger ships of the fleet and the treasure, while Blake stayed out through the winter to maintain the blockade and await the arrival of the next Plate fleet. Blake's health was failing, the winter weather was bad and the fleet was running short of supplies, but in February 1657 his patience was rewarded with the news that the Plate fleet was approaching.

His captains clamoured to give chase. Blake would have none of it. Twice he forestalled them. Only in April, when he was certain that the Spanish treasure ships were at anchor at Santa Cruz de Teneriffe in the Canary Islands, and that neither the Spanish battle fleet in Cadiz nor a visiting Dutch squadron under de Ruyter would go to their aid, did he give the order to abandon the blockade of the Spanish coast.

The Spanish ships were anchored under the guns of the shore forts. Blake used the same strategy he had employed at Porto Farina. He selected thirteen frigates to sail inshore to attack the ships, while the remainder of the fleet, including all the more powerful ships, engaged the guns of the shore forts. The captains asked that Stayner lead the attack.

The Spanish resistance was stiffer than that encountered at Porta Farina. Stayner's ships had to suffer withering fire as they carefully manoeuvred into position to make best use of the superior English gunnery. Once the English did open fire, they made short work of the smaller Spanish ships. The larger Spanish ships were soon caught in the crossfire of Stayner's inshore squadron and the main fleet under Blake in the bay. Systematically the remaining Spanish ships were boarded and set on fire.

It now remained for the inshore squadron to warp out against the wind. Against orders five captains attempted to leave with prizes. Three times Blake ordered them to desist before his order was obeyed and the Spanish ships were fired. All the English ships, many of them badly damaged managed to drag themselves to safety.
It was Blake's last and greatest victory. The entire Spanish squadron of sixteen ships was destroyed under the guns of their own shore forts, at a total cost of two hundred English killed and wounded. More importantly it was a victory for caution, clear planning and discipline. Blake left little to chance, and stubbornly resisted his captains' clamour to chase pell-mell in search of prizes. Earlier he had not the judgement or the control of his captains to achieve this. This was the mature Blake -authoritative and authoritarian - whom Nelson (who, be it remembered, tried the same attack on Santa Cruz and failed) admired.

In July the dying man was allowed to return home. His one wish was to set foot on English soil once more. Though his ship the *George* was diverted to Plymouth, the old man was not to get his wish. He died as his ship entered Plymouth Sound, issuing instructions to the last to help his comrades left tossing off the coast of Spain. Secretary of State Thurloe wrote:

"A very worthy and brave man is gone and a faithful servant of his Highness."

His body was embalmed and carried on his nephew's ship to Greenwich to lie in state. From here it was taken up the Thames to London for a grand state funeral and buried in King Henry VII's Chapel in Westminster Abbey amongst the great and good of the Commonwealth, only to be disinterred with them after the Restoration.

A solitary, shy man, who only relaxed in the presence of a few familiar friends, his many letters are those of a man of action obsessed with getting things done. He could never play the courtier, but could write with authority to kings. He never married and was uneasy in the presence of women. A devoted public servant, his work was his testament. He never betrayed the confidence his various public masters placed in him. His relationship with his wayward captains was sometimes tempestuous, but his men loved him. A devout man, he died at peace with his Lord.

During the Interregnum the English Navy established itself as a world power. The organisation for the future was laid out; the traditions were set. And central to all that was Robert Blake.

CHAPTER 2 BLAKE'S OFFICERS

The Council of State issued commissions for flag officers and captains - in practice the appointments were made by the Admiralty Committee (Admiralty Commissioners after 1653). Only when replacements were needed during a cruise did Blake appoint men directly (**2.1 and 2.2.**). However Blake and other admirals regularly used their influence to secure the appointment of men they thought worthy (**2.3**) and the Admiralty Commission (of which, as a General at Sea, Blake was a member) relied on these recommendations. Such was the rapid expansion of the Navy in the early stages of the Commonwealth that suitable men were at a premium. The criteria for appointment seem to have been principally religious zeal, commitment to the cause, and bravery (**2.4**). Navigational skill was not a pre-requisite - the sailing of the ship could be left to the master - and several army officers were appointed. Nevertheless there were probably a higher proportion of skilled navigators amongst the Commonwealth captains, since many (the "tarpaulins") had been commanders of merchant ships (like Vice Admirals Richard Badiley and John Lawson). Blake's judgement of character was sometimes challenged as **2.5 and 2.6** show. On larger ships a lieutenant assisted the captain - again with a commission from the Council of State. Such men were sometimes entrusted with important confidential messages (**6.14**) and often received their first promotion as a commander of a captured prize (**2.7**).

In charge of the sailing and navigation of a warship was a professional seaman - the **master**. Captains had considerable influence in the appointment of their master, since the latter's local knowledge of the seas in which the ships would operate was very important since there were no accurate navigational charts. Many such were former masters of merchant ships, or former naval captains. In an emergency senior dockyard managers might be called upon to fill this role (**2.8**).

The day-to-day running of the ship was in the hands of a number of **warrant officers**, all of whom were responsible for ordering and accounting for stores. Many of them held office in the same ship for years, though the new Generals, to judge by the number of warrants they issued in the Spring of 1649, seem to have been determined to see reliable men in post. Promotion was usually from the lower decks and from one ship to a better and Blake knew many personally **(2.9 and 2.10)**.

Boatswains were responsible for the routine running of the ship - for ropes, sails, anchors and communicating the routine orders of the senior officers to the men **(2.9 and 2.16)**.

During a battle or after a storm it was usually the skill and ingenuity of the **carpenter** that kept the ship afloat. There were always repairs to be made and stores to be managed. The rapid expansion of the Navy involved the recruitment of more suitable men. For this the Admiralty Committee looked for advice to a committee of merchants **(2.10 and 2.11)**. English iron naval cannon were the best in Europe at the time, and good **gunners** to maintain them were at a premium **(2.12 and 2.13)**.

No officer was more susceptible to accusations of embezzlement than the **purser**, for it was he who ordered and accounted for the food and drink on the ship. Apparently corruption was routine. Often pursers were landsmen with accounting skills and they could be given special assignments **(2.15)**. Sometimes they understood enough of the sea to become captains **(2.14)**.

Midshipmen were young men who had already learned some of the specialist tasks of the management of the ship and could look forward to further promotion **(2.16)**. Reliable older men often filled the office of **cook (2.17)**.

Surgeons were often appointed from a list kept by the London Company of Barber Surgeons. Blake formed personal attachments to those who served as surgeons on his flagships **(2.18 and 2.19)**. Arguably the appointment of **chaplain** was one of the most important on the ship, such was the store that devout admirals like Blake put on the spiritual life of the fleet (**2.20**). Chaplains were expected to preach regularly, though because of the diversity of religious viewpoints at the time it was not unknown for a captain out of sympathy with his chaplain also to preach. All flag officers would also have at least one **clerk** (**2.21**).

2.1 Blake to Captain John Stoakes, commander of the Unicorn

Whereas Captain Joseph Jordan, Rear Admiral of the fleet, hath obtained my leave to repair to England about some extraordinary business whereby that place is vacant. These are therefore to authorise you in his stead to act as Rear Admiral of the fleet, and further to put up and wear a Jack flag on the mizzen topmast head of the ship under your command until further order. And all commanders, officers, seamen and others with the fleet belonging are hereby strictly charged and required to take notice thereby in their respects and duties accordingly. For which this shall be your warrant.

> *On board the George in Castcais Road this first day of September 1655.*
S.P. 18. 118. 9*.

2.2 Blake and Deane to the Navy Commissioners

The Council of State having ordered the putting forth to sea in the present expedition of the ship Saint Cleer, with the Warspite, and Galliott Hoy, in lieu of merchant ships; we have appointed Commanders to serve them for the Saint Cleer Samuel Howett, Warspite William Wheatley, Galliot Hoy, Richard Pittocke....

> *Westminster 6 April 1649.*
S.P. 18. 1. 45*.

2.3 Blake and Penn to the Admiralty and Navy Commissioners

We are informed that the 5th rate frigate at Southampton is in such a forwardness as to entertain officers, and therefore we do recommend unto you, Capt. James Terry now in the Great Charity to be commander of her, and for other officers we shall supply out of the fleet if we have your concurrence.....

> *Swiftsure in Stoakes Bay the 3 of March 1653.*
S.P. 18. 80. 11*.

2.4 Blake and Monck to the Admiralty Commissioners

....We have this morning sent away the Foresight[1] frigate for Chatham, being very foul and wanting a new foremast which could not be supplied here.... The captain of her is a godly and valiant man, whom with Captain Newbury, commander of the Entrance, we do especially recommend for two of the best frigates now a building which, if you shall approve and appoint unto, we shall deliver them commissions upon notice given..... There are two honest captains more whom we desire to recommend unto you for removal into some of the new frigates now in building with good strength, viz. Capt. Blagg in the Marmaduke and Captain Hermon in the Welcome. They are already in ships of good force but slow sailors, and do not apprehend they would do more and better service if better provided....

Resolution off of Winterton, the 4th July, 1653.

S.P. 38. 7*.

1   Transcribed by Powell as *"Forester"*. The un-named captain was Richard Stayner, later the hero of Santa Cruz. Richard Newbury was a well known religious zealot - a reputed Anabaptist, twice imprisoned after the Restoration. Edward Blagg was another religious radical.

2.5 Blake and Penn to the Admiralty Commissioners

....Here is one Captain John Jeffries, commander of the Little Charity, who is an active man and well reported for an honest man, and therefore have thought to propose him unto you for Commander of the 4th frigate now building at Bristol....

Swiftsure in Ellen Road 14th Feb 1654

S.P. 18. 79. 87*.

2.6   Blake and Mountagu to the Admiralty Commissioners

....We have received your letter with the information against Captain Jeffries[1] and his Purser....which we have not yet had time to examine, but shall with the first conveniency....

March 9th 1656

Admiral Blake Museum MSS*.

1.   Jeffries was a religious radical, and a gallant officer who was accused of fraud and mismanagement by his cook. Convicted of fraud, he escaped with a small fine and continued to serve until the end of the Interregnum.

2.7   Blake and Monck to the Admiralty Commissioners

The bearer Edward Morecock[1], Lt of this ship being an honest and valiant man, of whose experience in this and other engagements we can testify very well, and therefore have thought fit to grant him a commission to be commander of one of the Dutch prizes lately taken, called the Elias of Amsterdam, we desire she may be one of the first that is fitted out amongst them, being informed she is a very good sailor.....

The Resolution off the Texel 9th June 1653

S.P. 18. 37. 62*

1.   Edward Morecock (or Moorcock) was a Baptist who continued to preach after the Restoration.

2.8   Blake and Penn to the Generals of the Fleet

We understand that the Sovereign is careened[1] on both sides and on Monday next will be ready to take in provisions, but no master is yet come down to take charge of her whose care will be much concerned in seeing the provisions stowed, as well as the expediting of her to sea likewise, and not knowing any person so fit for that employment as Mr Arkinstall[2] we do desire you will lay your commands upon him, that he forthwith makes his repair to Portsmouth to take the said charge upon him, whose presence will be of very much concernment for the reasons above said, also that he will bring as many able men as he can procure along with him of which that ship will very much want.

Swiftsure in Stokes Bay the 17 of Feb. 1654.

S.P. 18. 9. 123*.

1.   Drawn out of the water and the bottom scraped clean of marine growth.
2.   Thomas Arkinstall was Master Attendant at the dockyard at Chatham. On several occasions he was sent to sea as master in some of the more important ships - the *Sovereign* was the largest ship in the fleet.

2.9   Blake and Deane to the Navy Commissioners

Whereas we have formerly given you a warrant for the ordering of Elias Mitchell, late Boatswain of the ship Greyhound, to be removed into the Henrietta Maria; and forasmuch as we are informed of the fidelity of John London to be a present servant of the Commonwealth and also his ability to operate the place of Boatswain in the said ship Greyhound; these are to authorise you ......

Westminster 6th April 1649

S.P. 18. 6. 9

2.10   Petition of Hopkins and Blake's reply

To the Right Honourable Col. Robert Blake, Admiral and General of the fleet, The humble petition of William Hopkins Carpenter, Showeth That your petitioner hath served the Parliament ever since the beginning of these troubles and for his faithful discharging thereof and ability therein he hath certificates to manifest the same.   And whereas your Honour was graciously pleased to promise your petitioner a removal to some more likely vessel whereby your petitioner may be better encouraged to venture his life and fortunes, having a charge of wife and children and finding little encouragement where he now is. Do therefore humbly implore your Honour to vouchsafe him a removal into one of the new frigates as

21

shall seem best pleasing to your Honour. And your petitioner as in duty bound shall ever pray etc.

The petitioner having for a long time served at the Navy Yard whereof as a carpenter in the Victory and being one of whom I have formerly had in consideration as a person deserving a better ship it is therefore humbly desired that the Commissioners of the Admiralty and Navy will look upon him as a man fit to be removed into the frigate building by Mr. Taylor at Wapping or some other good vessel as to your Honours shall seem meet.

Chatham 10th January 1653.

S.P. 18. 45 69*.

2.11   Blake to the Navy Commissioners

Forasmuch as I am informed that the place of Master Gunner in the frigate called the Little Elizabeth is now vacant by the removal of the late Gunner thereof; these are therefore to authorise, and desire you to give order that Edward Larkyn be entered Gunner of the said frigate till further order with such allowance of wages, and diet for himself, and servant, as is usual in a vessel of her quality....

Whitehall 2nd December 1651

Messrs Maggs MSS.

2.12   Blake and Mountagu to the Admiralty Commissioners

....Considering the character you give of Reader, we are not very free to part with him at this season, as not showing readily how to supply the present place he hath so well, and intending ourselves with the first opportunity to remove him to be gunner of a better ship, or else some other way prefer him....

Naseby 10 March 1656

Add. MSS. B.M. 20085,2*.

22

2.13   Blake and Deane to the Navy Commissioners

Whereas the ship Victory now fitting forth to sea is destitute of a Carpenter, William Boarman the late carpenter being ejected by the Act of Parliament, forasmuch as the Committee of Merchants for regulating the Navy have recommended Arthur Pembroke carpenter of the Fellowship as a fit man to operate that place, these are to desire you to give order that the said Arthur Pembroke be entered as carpenter of the said ship the Victory, with such allowances of wages and diet, for himself and his servant as is usual in a ship of her quality; and this shall be your warrant.

5th April 1649.

S.P. 18. 6. 7.

2.14   Blake and Deane to the Navy Commissioners

Whereas the place of purser in the Truelove frigate is now vacant by the removal of John Gossage into the Recovery, and forasmuch as William Crispin[1] hath been recommended for a faithful man to manage such an employment; These are to desire you to give order that the said William Crispin....be entered purser of the said frigate Truelove with such allowance of wages and diet for himself and his servant as is usual in a vessel of her quality; And this shall be your warrant.

3rd April 1649

S.P. 18. 6. 2.

1.   William Crispin later became a captain and served under Penn in the "Western Design".

2.15   Blake to the Navy Commissioners

The purser's place in the Resolution being vacant by the removal of Phineas Pett[1] to be assistant to the Master Shipwright at Chatham, and having had long experience of the faithfulness of Thomas Lewis now purser of the Speaker frigate who during the being of the State's fleet then under my command before Lisbon appeared very forward to further the public service, adventuring himself several times through the enemies' fleet with letters to the Agent, and was afterwards employed to victual the fleet on the coast of Spain, upon which consideration together with his long service in the Navy and his pains in the distribution of the victualling of the fleet all the last summer and last winter; ....that if your Honours shall think fit he may .... remove into the said ship Resolution, which as I doubt not but he will discharge with faithfulness....

Triumph, 9th December 1652

S.P. 18. 39. 112*.

1.   Phineas Pett was a member of the famous shipbuilding family whose brother, Peter Pett was a Navy Commissioner. He served in at least two ships as purser and held a variety of administrative posts in dockyards. The *Resolution* was the second largest ship in the fleet and the position of purser would have been lucrative.

2.16   Blake and Penn to the Admiralty Commissioners

....We desire to recommend unto you for officers in the great new frigates at Woolwich the persons following, viz: Thomas May, midshipman here, for Boatswain of the 4th rate frigate at Bristol....

Swiftsure in Ellen Road the 18th March, 1653.

S.P. 18. 68. 2*.

2.17   Blake and Penn to the Admiralty and Navy Commissioners

The bearer Joseph Walters was servant to Genl Deane in his life time by the space of 4 or 5 years and being recommended unto us for an honest, and fit person to discharge the office and place of cook in one of the new frigates. We have therefore thought necessary to recommend him unto you for cook in such one of the new frigates if you shall think fit, his certificates we have sent here enclosed....

Swiftsure in Ellen Road the 6th March 1654

S.P. 18. 80. 65*.

2.18   Blake to the Navy Commissioners

I have been desired by John Halstock[1] surgeon (who hath gone along with me in several ships) to write unto you that the place in the Worcester frigate may be reserved for him; ever since I took charge at sea I have by myself and others observed his great care, and diligence especially in the last expedition to the southward....I therefore desire you to give order that the said place may not be disposed of to another....

Portland Road 27 September 1651

S.P. 18. 17. 86*.

1.   Halstock, whom Blake twice recommended, was of a higher calibre than many surgeons.   An Oxford graduate he was chosen to embalm Cromwell's body.

2.19   Blake and Penn to the Navy Commissioners

The Sovereign being destined for the next summer's guard, and being informed that she will be ready to sail in about 3 weeks hence we have appointed Mr. Matthew Linde[1] chirugeon of her, and thought necessary to send him up to London herewith, that he might furnish his chest with physical drugs and medicaments suitable to a ship of that rank ....

Swiftsure in Stokes Bay 21 Feb. 1654

S.P. 18. 66. 71.

1   Matthew Linde was a friend of Blake's and was one of the witnesses of his will.   Surgeon on the *George* when Blake died, he embalmed the body.

2.20   Blake to the Navy Commissioners

The bearer Mr. Wickcot is very well recommended unto me for an able and godly minister to go along with me this present expedition, and being by reason of the shortness of time and absence of his friends unable to furnish himself with moneys for making provision necessary to such a voyage, I make it my request unto you That you will be pleased to advance twenty pounds by way of imprest unto him that he may speedily fit himself for the service .....

Aboard the George in the Hope, 24 Jul: 1654.

Addit. MSS 19367,4*.

2.21 Order of Blake and Admiralty Commissioners

That the Commissioners of the Navy do make out a bill unto Mr. William Simpson for the pay, entertainment due unto him as chief clerk to Gen. Blake in his late expedition to the Straits, and as deputy treasurer to the squadron under his command from the 7th day of July 1654 to the time the ship is paid off, after the rate of £200 per annum.

22 January 1656

S.P. 18. 132. 127

CHAPTER 3 BLAKE'S MEN

Such was the massive expansion of the Navy during the Commonwealth period, particularly during the Anglo-Dutch War, that Blake and his fellow commanders were always short of sailors to man the fleet. Where possible volunteers were recruited – a share in the prize money from a captured ship was a significant incentive. Yet even after the pay of seamen had been raised at Blake's insistence after the Battle of Dungeness, the pay in the merchant service was usually higher, and there was a steady drain away from the ships of war (**3.1**).

Throughout the period, to make up the numbers, men were pressed to service. In theory any seaman (in practice any adult under the age of sixty living in a seaport) who was not already bound to a ship could be made to serve. The authorities in the ports were regularly ordered to press quotas of men, giving each man 12 pence (known in later times as "the King's shilling") and conduct money (**3.2**). The ports seldom raised anything like their expected quotas. It was sometimes more effective to give warrants to particular captains to press men directly for their own ships (**3.3**). Frequently the men who were pressed had no experience of the sea or were very young (**3.4**). Those that were pressed often contrived to escape on the journey to their ship, so ships would be sent to collect them (**3.4**). Even this was sometimes in vain (**3.6**).

An expedient was to take seamen from one warship to man another, either by paying men off early (**3.7**) or depleting the crew of several ships to provide a crew for another (**3.8**). Sometimes soldiers were seconded to sea service, not simply to act as marines, but also to help sail the ships (**3.9**). Generally soldiers did not make good sailors (**3.10**). Recruits in general often needed to be provided for (**3.11**). Whilst still in port sailors often took the opportunity to desert and the port authorities were commissioned to apprehend them (**3.12**).

Pay was a frequent cause of friction. The pay in the navy was lower than in the merchant service (and lower than in neighbouring continental navies). Prize money, the main attraction of naval service, was often slow in being paid **(3.13)**. Blake did succeed in getting the pay of seamen increased in 1653, but still it was frequently in arrears **(3.15)**. It was the cause of the discontent in the navy during the winter of 1655-6.

The method of payment often caused hardship. At the end of a cruise seamen were given a ticket signed by the captain of their ship. These could only be cashed at the offices of the Navy Commissioners in London, so, if the ship was paid off in Plymouth, mariners had a long journey to cash their tickets. This led to the practice of middlemen buying up tickets (at a discount) and travelling to London to cash them wholesale. Officially this practice was frowned on, but Blake had the humanity and pragmatism to see that such practices were to the benefit of the men **(3.14)**. He also petitioned for the seamen's families in real need to be allowed pay tickets in advance of ships being paid off **(3.16)**.

3.1   Blake and Penn to the Admiralty Commissioners

We find that notwithstanding all our care to provide men for the fleet we do not only come short of our expectations, but many of those we have do also desert the service, although all due care hath been taken for prevention thereof, which it is conceived is chiefly occasioned by that general liberty given to merchants' men going to sea, not so safe, according to the present state of affairs, for we are informed that there is gone out of the western ports of this nation at least 3000 able seamen, this last eastwardly wind which we fear will be very much wanted to man this next summer's guard.

Swiftsure in Stokes Bay, 17 Feb. 1654

S.P. 18. 79. 116*.

Plate III Vice Admiral John Lawson

The doyen of the "tarpaulin" captains of the Commonwealth, Lawson was a former shipmaster of a Newcastle collier and fought as an infantry officer in the Civil War. He was appointed a naval captain at the beginning of the Commonwealth, and distinguished himself in several battles in the First Anglo-Dutch War. Popular with the ordinary seamen, he had the reputation of being a political and religious radical and appeared to champion the cause of discontent in the Navy in 1656. Cromwell saw him as a threat and posted him as Vice Admiral to Blake in the Spanish expedition to try to limit his influence. Rather than sail, Lawson resigned and subsequently became involved with moves to restore the King. Knighted at the Restoration he died fighting in the Second Anglo-Dutch War.

[Admiral Blake Museum]

Plate IV Model of a Great Ship of the Commonwealth period

A 1st rate ship of 92 guns.

[Admiral Blake Museum]

3.2 Blake and Lambert to the Mayor and Jurats of Rye

There being a very great want of able mariners to furnish the fleet now setting forth to sea for the defence and service of the Commonwealth, we have thought it expedient to direct these our letters to you authorizing and requiring you that forthwith on receipt hereof you do impress and raise within your town and the members thereof, sixty able seamen, being above the age of fifteen and under sixty giving each man so by you to be raised twelve pence press money and three half pence a mile conduct from the place where they shall be impressed to the Town of Dover.   And you are to order them to make their immediate repair before the Mayor of the said Town unto whom we have written to take care for the sending them on board the State's ships in the Downs.   And you are to transmit unto the Commissioners for the Admiralty a true and perfect list of the names of such persons as you shall hereupon impress and of the places of their abode together with an account of your expenses.....

Whitehall 19th January 1656.

Corporation of Rye MSS*.

3.3 Blake and Deane to Penn

By virtue of the power derived unto us as Admiral and General of the Fleet, these are to authorise you from time to time as there shall be occasion, to press mariners for completing the number borne upon the ship under your command, according to an Act of Parliament in that behalf; provided that the persons by you to be employed to press men, be such as for their fair carriage therein you will answer; and to be careful and tender in pressing of mariners out of ships outwards bound; and this shall be your warrant.

Westminster 11th April 1649

Portland Papers*.

3.4   Blake and Deane to the Admiralty Commissioners

....Just now the Lieutenant of this ship cometh to inform us that there are a few imprest men come aboard that have never been to sea, and are very boys, by which means you are deceived, when you think they send us seamen, and the service cannot but suffer if there be not greater care taken, they tell us that they were pressed by the Masters of Waterman's Hall....

From aboard the Triumph in Dover Road 12th February 1653.

Admiral Blake Museum MSS*.

3.5   Blake to the Mayor of Sandwich

Captain Rowan informs me that he has pressed sixteen men of the Town of Sandwich and there being occasion for their speedy repair hither; I have sent this vessel to receive them and their Clothes, and desire you would command some of your officers to see the said persons sent away.....

Downs 17th June 1652

Sandwich Corporation MSS.*

3.6   Blake to the Navy Commissioners

We are in great straits for want of men although we have drenched these parts and for further recru(its) I am necessitated to order the Victory into Lee Road, and send the Nightingale, and Nonsuch ketch for the coast of Suffolk, there to press what they can....

Downs 28 March 1652

S.P. 18. 27. 60*.

3.7   Order by Blake and the Admiralty Commissioners

Whereas it is held requisite that the Mariners belonging to the Assistance be forthwith turned over into the Worcester in order to her speedy getting to sea; It is therefore ordered, that it be referred to the Commissioners and Treasurer for the Navy to pay off the said ship's company their wages upon their removal into the Worcester, reserving 3 months thereof in the States hands.

20 Dec. 1655.

S.P. 18. 18. 125.

3.8   Blake and Penn to the Admiralty Commissioners

Yours of the 16th instant we received, and the same day did arrive here the Martin, Merlin, Drake and Nonsuch ketch, out of whom we took as many men as they could (?) towards manning the Sovereign and have remanded them to their former stations, the Martin only excepted....

Swiftsure in Ellen Road the 18th March, 1653.
S.P. 18. 68. 2*.

3.9   Blake and Penn to the Admiralty Commissioners

By yours of the 4th instant we perceive that the treaty is still very uncertain, so that 1000 land soldiers are appointed to repair to Portsmouth for manning the fleet if occasion be; which are too few to answer our necessity, and therefore desire that 500 or 1000 able soldiers more may be hastened unto us, which will no more than enable us for service, so far as we can discern.....

Swiftsure in Ellen Road March 7, 1654.
S.P. 18. 67 .35*.

3.10   Blake and Monck to the Navy Commissioners

....and whereas you desire our opinion about taking Soldiers a Shipboard, we hold it at this time of the year to be very unseasonable, and of little advantage to the service they being unprovided of all conveniences and not able (as we have found by experience) to brook this winter weather....

Chatham 16 January 1653
R.C. Anderson MSS*.

3.11   Blake and Monck to the Admiralty Commissioners

....We have also sent in the Ruby frigate about twenty six men whom we desire you will give order to be carefully looked after. The seamen and soldiers especially are in great want of clothes some having hardly wherewithal to cover their nakedness, and therefore desire you will think of some speedy course to supply us in that particular.

Resolution off of the Texel the 20th June 1653.
S.P. 18. 37. 121*.

3.12 Blake to the Mayor of Sandwich

I am informed that divers Mariners belonging to the fleet under my command have lately got ashore and doe obscure themselves in several Towns within your precinct to the great disservice of the Commonwealth: My desire therefore unto you is that you would give strict charge to your several deputies that they forthwith make diligent search in the places they belong unto for all Mariners, and other concerned herein. And such as they find to send immediately hither as also that none be permitted either to pass through your precinct or be entertained without they have Certificate under my hand and seal of the Anchor. Herein I doubt not of your readiness, it so much tending to the good of the present service.

Downs, 29th May 1652.

Admiral Blake Museum MSS. D83.

3.13 Abstract of a letter from Blake

....(my) loss of seamen is extraordinary, and unless there be speedy care taken in paying them off their money, and furnishing out new assistance, we shall be but in a sad condition. For indeed they cry out extremely for money, and refuse to engage again gratis, whereas the enemy give their men their prizes and 40s a month; ours have no allowance of prizes and but 18s a month. This sticks in their stomachs and quells their valour, which otherwise might prove happily instrumental in the good of this nation.

December 7 1652.

French Occurrences, p.220. B.M.E., 683, 26*.

34

3.14   Blake to the Navy Commissioners

There have been this summer divers mariners prest in this and other Western ports into the State's ships; and in respect of their habitations are so far distant from London, many of them have, upon going in of the ships that they served in, been discharged here; and one Mr. Edward Pattison of this town, out of charity hath paid them their tickets, they being poor people and not able to look after it alone; this man acquaints me that for some tickets notwithstanding he has been without his money a good while, is in danger to lose it through delay. I know not what the reason is but I believe what he did was merely to relieve and ease the poor men. I therefore make it my desire to you that you will give order for the payment of such tickets as he hath or shall present to you....

Plymouth 28 August 1651.

S.P. 18. 17. 69*.

3.15   Blake to the Navy Commissioners

Complaint hath been made unto me that the wages of John Beale, Boatswain of the Elizabeth frigate, were at her paying off at Portsmouth stopped, and so remain, upon what pretence I know not and in regard that frigate is gone to the South ward, and the petitioner still in execution of the duty of his place, nothing of misdemeanour, nor of fraudulency, appearing that might occasion such a stop, I desire you....to order payment of the wages due....

Whitehall 21st January 1652.

S.P. 18. 27. 13*.

3.16   Blake to Secretary Thurloe

....I have been induced in favour of divers poor seamen belonging to the fleet for relief of their families and relations to allow you making out some few tickets (not exceeding twenty) for each ship which I desire may be past and paid accordingly as soon as they come before you notwithstanding any order to the contrary....

George off Cape Vincent the 6th July 1655.

Middleton Blake MSS*.

Plate V The Triumph

This drawing by Willem van de Velde the Elder is dated 1661, i.e. just after the Restoration. The Triumph, a Second Rate built in 1623 mounting up to 74 guns,

was Blake's first flagship in 1649 and flew his flag in the Battles of Dungeness and Portland in the Anglo-Dutch War. [Boymans van Beuningen Museum, Rotterdam]

CHAPTER 4 BLAKE'S SHIPS

The Navy which Blake and his colleagues took over in 1649 consisted of a number of dedicated warships - the State Ships - and a larger number of hired armed merchant ships. During the Interregnum there was a massive expansion of the fleet, partly as a result of a huge shipbuilding programme and partly through the assimilation into the Navy of captured prizes, particularly former Dutch warships (**3.7**).

Some of the State Ships which Blake inherited dated back to the reign of King James and were large, old fashioned and slow. In addition there were the ships built with Ship Money in the 1630s, the most famous of which and the largest was the *Sovereign*. Though one of the grandest ships in Europe of her time, she had limited usefulness and seems to have spent much of the period out of commission. Significantly, Blake never flew his flag in her. In the Battle of the Kentish Knock she went aground, but once refloated reputedly took on twenty Dutch ships. The problems of getting the *Sovereign* to sea are illustrated in **Nos.4.1-4.3**.

Lighter armed frigates were generally used for convoy work and scouting. In 1649 they were often hired merchant ships which had been equipped for war (**4.4**). Subsequently a new design of large, fast, flush decked frigates were developed which, in addition to convoy and scouting, were sufficiently heavily armed to be used in fleet actions. It was these Fourth Rates that played a crucial role in the Battles of Porto Farina and Santa Cruz.

Armed merchant ships were also used at the beginning of the Commonwealth period in large fleet actions, though this practice was discontinued after Blake found them unreliable at the Battle of Dungeness. Armed merchant ships continued to be used for convoy work, as supply ships and as fire ships (**4.5 and 4.6**). Small hired merchant ships - ketches and hoys - were used throughout the Interregnum as tenders for the large state ships, for scouting, and anonymously, for spying (**4.7 - 4.9**).

All ships carried extra men in time of war - such additional men had to be paid and fed - and this caused problems for naval administration (**4.10 and 4.11**). Sometimes individual captains cut through red tape and used their own money to get ships ready for sea (**4.12**). Even when the additional men and supplies were obtained, there was still additional equipment to be got such as studding sails to give ships more speed(**4.13**) and small arms for hand-to-hand combat in boarding parties (**4.14**).

4.1   Blake and Penn to the Admiralty Commissioners

Yours of the 16th and 18th with another of the 21st present we received, whereby we understand that care is being taken for furnishing the Sovereign with a lower tier of ordnance which she will be ready to receive so soon as they can be sent down, and therefore desire the more expedition may be used.

Swiftsure in Stoakes Bay, the 25th Feb. 1653.

S.P. 18. 66. 71

4.2   Blake and Penn to the Admiralty and Navy Commissioners

Yours of the 28 of last month we received, and understand that the lower tier of ordnance for the Sovereign is shipped aboard a vessel for Portsmouth which cannot come sooner than expected she being ready for them, but yet we shall suspend her coming out of the harbour, till we have your approbation and therefore desire your answer by the next. For a supply of men, we shall much rejoice in, if what you have in expectation will answer this service.

Swiftsure in Stoakes Bay the 3 of March 1653.

S.P. 18. 80. 11*.

4.3   Blake and Penn to the Admiralty Commissioners

Yesterday we got the Sovereign into Stokes Bay, where all endeavours shall be used to enable her for service, as well as the rest of the fleet....

Swiftsure in Ellen Road the 14th March 1653.

S.P. 18. 67. 81.

4.4   Blake and Popham to the Navy Commissioners

We understand that you have contracted with Daniel Rosewel for the Mary frigate to be employed in this present expedition; it is therefore our desire, that you would give present order for her fitting with victuals and stores, according to the Contract....

Westminster 16th March 1649

R.C. Anderson MSS.

4.5   Blake and Deane to the Navy Commissioners

The Council of State having ordered the putting forth to sea in the present expedition of the ship Saint Cleer, with the Warspite, and Galliott Hoy, in lieu of merchant ships...we earnestly desire you to issue your warrants forthwith to the master shipwright for performing what carpenter's work is required to be done upon them, as also that order may be given for their fitting with carpenter's and boatswain stores, we having authorised the officers to go aboard them for better furtherance of their hastening out. We likewise desire a speedy course to be taken for victualling the said vessels may not after they are fitted stay for want therof....

Westminster 6 April 1649.

S.P. 18. 1. 45*.

4.6   Order by Blake and the Admiralty Commissioners

That the Fox and Little President be forthwith fitted up to serve as fireships, as the Hope flyboat and Marigold to carry supplies of provisions for the use of the fleet now setting forth and the Commissioners for the Navy are to take effectual order therein accordingly; for which this shall be their warrant.

S.P. 18. 132. 43   *8 January 1656..*

4.7   Blake and Deane to the Navy Commissioners

The Rebecca ketch being contracted for by you to serve the fleet in this expedition; and now specially assigned by us to attend the Triumph and other ships coming in Tilbury Hope, as soon as they shall be fitted to put forth to sea, we desire you to give order that she may be speedily victualled for 3 months for 16 men, the captain affirming she cannot conveniently stow a greater proportion.... as before.   *Westminster 6th April 1649.*
S.P. 18. 1. 44*.

4.8   Order by Blake and the Admiralty Commissioners

That the Commissioners for the Navy do renew their contract for the Adventure ketch, to attend the Resolution, and to provide ketches for every other ship of the fleet and second rate of the fleet, designed for the Straits, to assist them in the impressing of men and to be continued in the service as long as the State shall have occasion ....   *January 1 1656.*
S.P. 18. 132. 1.

4.9   Blake to the Admiralty Commissioners

To the Commissioners of the Admiralty Cuthbert Embleton hath served the State with his hoy the Speedwell according to contract from the 17th day of December 1653 to the 30th day of August 1654, and was then discharged having no further occasion to employ the vessel. Dated aboard the George in the Downs the day and year last above mentioned.
S.P. 18. 87. 49*.
Note. Embleton and his vessel were employed as a spy on the coast of Holland.

4.10   Blake and Deane to the Navy Commissioners

Whereas the Council of State hath ordered 20 pieces of iron ordnance to be put aboard the ship Concord and whereas your certificates mention but 65 men to be borne on her; we having taken into consideration that number will be too few for her in the present service do desire you to give order that 15 men more be added with allowance of victuals accordingly....

                      Dated at Westminster the 17 of April 1649.
S.P. 18. 6. 18*.

4.11   Blake to the Navy Commissioners

The Commander of the Weymouth pink being very speedily to go upon service with that vessel informs me that the Clerks of Dockyard at Deptford notwithstanding there is victuals aboard her for 70 men four months refuse to enter any more than 60. My desire unto you is, in respect that frigate may happily meet with some opposition in her convoying vessels to and again; That you would issue your order to the Captain for the completing the said number....

Whitehall, 13th Jan. 1652.

S.P. 18. 27. 9*.

4.12   Blake to the Navy Commissioners

Some days since there was by special order from the Comm^{rs} of the Admiralty, ten men added to the Recovery, and by letter from Capt. Chapman dated the 13th instant I am informed that the victualler at Portsmouth refuseth to deliver any more provisions than according to her former complement....I have one more thing to commend unto you which is that in respect Captain Stoakes hath been much out of purse for supplies since repaid in sails, and rigging if not only for himself but others of his squadron, that you would favour him so far as to give credit to such bills as he chargeth in that nature, the disbursements appearing just and reasonable....

Chatham, 15 March 1652.

S.P. 18. 27. 51*.

4.13   Blake and Deane to the Navy Commissioners

The Council of State not long since ordered the provision of studding and other sails for the ships of the fleet, and better to enable them to give chase; we .... desire you to send such sails as are ready for the ships abroad aboard the Triumph, whereby we may dispose of them when we meet with the fleet....

Westminster, 17 April, 1649.

S.P. 18. 1. 60*.

4.14   Blake and Deane to the Council of State

We having desired of the Committee to the Navy that they would furnish the officers of the ordinance with money to buy 20 pairs of pistols for every ship of the first rate that shall go out in this expedition, and also 40 hatchets, and for every second rate ship 15 pairs of pistols with 30 hatchets; for every third rate ship 10 pairs of pistols with 20 hatchets, and for every smaller ship 8 pairs of pistols and 16 hatchets, without which weapons our men shall enter aboard the ship, they being unarmed men can do little service. We therefore humbly desire you will give order to the officers of the ordnance that this proportion may be delivered respectively to each ship according to the rates above mentioned....

Westminster 29, March 1649.

S.P. 25. 123. 27*.

CHAPTER 5 LIFE AT SEA

The availability of the right supplies of the right quality in the right quantities was a constant source of frustration to Blake and his fellow admirals and frequently hampered their freedom of action. Ships were fitted out in port either to the extent of the planned cruise or to the capacity of their holds. Generally this was adequate, though there were problems during the Dutch War, such were the demands of the fleet. It is almost certain that fortunes were made from supplying the fleet and attempts were made to make the process more efficient. John Disbrowe was appointed General at Sea in 1653 to oversee the administration and special Naval Commissioners were posted to ports to supervise supply. Trusted figures of the establishment like Colonel Pride were given contracts to supply (**6.9**). All things considered, by the standards of the time and the scale of naval activity during the Interregnum, the system managed just to keep pace with the needs of the fleet, and was a great deal better than in previous periods.

However, the problems of fitting out ships were compounded by the new demands of maintaining fleets at sea in distant stations for long periods. With the problems of communication, the profiteering and the perennial government shortage of money, Blake, at sea in some far off winter swell could be forgiven for thinking "out of sight was out of mind" (**5.30 & 5.31**).
With the enormous expenditure of ammunition in the Dutch War, supplies of gunpowder and shot were at a premium (**5.1**), and sometimes one ship was robbed to supply another (**5.2**). Even basic items had to be specially requisitioned (**5.3**). The supply of carpenters' and boatswains' stores could also present problems, since ships at sea had to be regularly maintained to remain seaworthy, and battles and storms inevitably took a heavy toll (**5.4 - 5.7**).

A seaman's diet consisted of ships biscuit, dried peas, salt pork and salt beef, with butter and cheese when it could be obtained (**5.8**). Such items were stowed for long voyages and, provided they were preserved, dried and stored correctly could last for months, but there were complaints (**5.9**). A supply of fresh meat was always welcome (**5.10**), though the quantities suggest only the officers benefitted. The arrival of victuallers - supply ships - was always eagerly anticipated (**5.11**). Even so these unimaginative rations did run short. The non-arrival of the victuallers led Blake to abandon his Mediterranean voyage in 1656.

More problematic on a long voyage was a supply of fresh water, used not only for drinking but also for soaking the salt out of the pork and beef. Salt beef soaked in salt water makes for a very salty diet and thirsty men. Usually men drank beer, which providing it had been correctly brewed and correctly stored, could keep for months. Unfortunately this did not always happen (**5.12 - 5.13**). On his long voyages Blake had resort to buying local wine - this presented problems because he had to be recompensed by the contractors in England. What they bought did not suit - it was too sweet (and thus not thirst quenching) and too strong (**5.14 - 5.15**). Blake gives a blunt assessment of the problems of supply on a long voyage - problems compounded by the venality of both the supply contractors and the pursers (**5.16**).

The confined conditions of life at sea, and the ever present danger of fire necessitated limits on the freedom of the crews and tight discipline (**5.17 - 5.18**). Storms could happen at any time, which in addition to causing damage dispersed the fleet (**5.19 - 5.20**) or caused collisions (**5.21**). Apart from seasickness (**5.22**), illness caused by bad food and bad water was endemic (**5.23 - 5.24**). During the Dutch Wars there were so many sick and injured men that they were regularly put ashore (**5.25 - 5.26**). The capture of numbers of Dutch ships also presented problems, since not only did the captured prizes have to be manned with English sailors (of whom there was always a shortage), but the captured prisoners had to be accommodated (**5.27**). The attitude of the men was generous - only a year after the end of the Dutch War they were volunteering deductions from their pay to ransom Dutch prisoners of the Moslems in North Africa (**5.28**). Long voyages took a toll on the health of and morale of the men and even on Blake himself (**5.29 - 5.30**).

5.1 Blake and Monck to the Navy Commissioners

....The proportion of powder and shot now in the fleet is not above 16 rounds to each gun, and we do apprehend that our want will not be less than 6 or 7000 barrels with shot proportionable to complete our former allowance and enable us for service. We do desire that 1000 barrels thereof and proportionable quantity of shot, or so much as you have at present, may be sent unto us in some of the nimblest frigates you have so soon as possibly you can; they shall find us plying as aforesaid. Our greatest want is shot, which we conceive is occasioned by the not sending a like proportion of both together, which inconvenience we desire for the future may be prevented....

S.P. 18. 37. 46   *From aboard the Resolution, June 6, 1653.*

5.2 Blake and Monck to the Admiralty and Navy Commissioners

The ship Ann and Joyce her victuals being ended and contract expired we have ordered her into the River and have taken out of her 16 barrels of powder and one hundred demi culverin round shot, and ninety four sakers for the use and service of the fleet, for which we have promised Captain Pyle commander of the said ship in the name of the State ready money for them at a reasonable price or else to have a like quantity of powder and shot restored to him at London....

S.P. 18. 55. 30*.   *Resolution the 21 of June 1653.*

5.3 Blake and Monck to the Admiralty Commissioners

....We hope you do not forget to send us paper and canvas for cartridges with a considerable quantity of junk for wads, our necessity in this particular having been several times made known unto you....

S.P. 38. 7*.   *Resolution off of Winterton, the 4th July, 1653.*

5.4 Blake and Mountagu to the Admiralty Commissioners

....We have disposed of the provisions of brasswork and carpenter's stores which came to us in the Endeavour and Thomas and Mary hoys, which doth yet answer each ships wants, especially cables and anchors which we desire may be thought on, and sent unto us....

Resolution at an anchor in Sole Bay, this 6th July, 1653.

S.P. 38. 19*.

5.5 Blake to Secretary Thurloe.

....The George is very leaky and her masts unsound. There is generally no small want of sails and canvas in the whole fleet with cordage and other things....

6 July 1655 Duplicate of this comes by the Mermaid

Rawlinson A. 39.195*.

5.6 Blake to the Admiralty Commissioners

....truly I cannot but wonder, if it be intended we must stay aboard so long time, that care is not likewise taken for supplying us with new stores,especially for boatswains' and carpenters', the Com^{rs} of the Navy being able to inform you that those we brought out with us from England cannot but be now much wasted and decayed; the more, considering (what I have often intimated) the turbulency of the weather we have found in these parts; insomuch that I may assure you there are very few ships in the fleet that have any more sails than what are at the yards, fit for service, and are not brought near to the like exigency for carpenters' stores, besides several other defects in most of them, especially in the great ships, and particularly the George, the head of her mainmast being sprung, and foremast unsound, the main yard defective, her hull is very leaky, and very little (if any) plank deals, nails, or other stores left to repair her, if yet that could be done here....

Aboard the George off Cape Vincent, 4th July 55.

Addit. MSS, 19367,9*.

5.7 Blake and Monck to the Navy Commissioners

....We understand some hammocks are come in a hoy to Harwich for which we have sent, but hear not of the other necessaries of wood and candles so often mentioned unto you of which the fleet wants a proportion of six weeks to even with our present victualling....

Aboard the Resolution, plying between the Vlie and the Texel, 12th June, 1653.

S.P. 37. 79*.

5.8 Blake and Monck to the Admiralty Commissioners

....We have still daily complaints about the defectiveness of victuals, especially beer, bread, butter and cheese....and that which adds to it is the loss of a hoy called the David, whose whole lading was bread, butter and cheese....We do not hear of any butter or cheese in these ships coming along with the Reserve.....

The Resolution plying between the Texel and the Vlie, 28th June 1653.

S.P. 37. 73*.

5.9 Blake and Monck to the Admiralty Commissioners

We have daily and renewed complaints of victuals, especially beer, and of this the beer in those victualling ships come along with the Reserve which we understand is generally very bad; but we have made it known to Col. Pride, now with us, who hath promised that a supply of better beer with other provisions shall be speedily sent us. However, we thought it necessary to acquaint you therewith that the like inconvenience for the future may be prevented and that a speedy supply of butter and cheese may be sent down to us.....
The next beer that come we desire some water may be sent along with it.

Resolution at an anchor in Sole Bay, this 6th July, 1653.
S.P. 38. 19*.

5.10 Blake to Penn

Mr. White, of Dover, hath provided at Deal 50 lbs of fresh beef for the fleet, which will be ready by tomorrow noon. I desire you will give order that one third thereof be fetched off and distributed among your squadron.

Downs, October 8, 1652 .

The Duke of Portland's MSS, Navy Papers, 1640-1696, fol.167*.

5.11   Blake to the Navy Commissioners?

... I presume you are sensible of the great expense we have made of our victuals by our so long stay here notwithstanding I have used all care and diligence in getting from this place what could be made ready, and have great reason to fear that much of what we have on board will prove defective being daily visited with complaints of that nature and having already found on board of several ships a considerable quantity of beef and pork altogether unserviceable, and some beer that stinketh which we received from this place.

George off Plymouth Sound, 9th of October 1654.

Addit. MSS. 9304. 95.

5.12   Blake and Monck to the Navy Commissioners

....We shall also desire that you will be pleased to mind the Victuallers of their promise of sending down one of themselves to see the disposing of what provisions comes hither which as yet is not by them performed, neither any effectual care taken therein, there being now 600 tons of Beer here all in wooden bound Cask which is not fit to be laid in the Ground Tiers and thereby not disposable of without prejudice to the service....

Chatham, 16th Janu: 53.

R.C. Anderson's MSS*.

5.13   Blake to the Admiralty Commissioners

....for furnishing ourselves with liquor, wherein yet we find much difficulty, that which doth not a little add thereunto being the want of iron bound casks.... It would have been much for the advantage of the service, if with the last victuals you had sent us two or three hundred tuns of beer, whereof I desire you will cause a good quality to be furnished with the next supplies, and the casks to be iron bound, the want of which (as I have mentioned before) hath been no small hindrance to our procuring drink hereabouts....

Aboard the George off Cape Vincent, 4th July 55.

Addit. MSS. 19367,9*.

5.14   Blake and Mountagu to the Admiralty Commissioners

....The Entrance and Hope flyboat found (it seems) by that time they came to the Madeiras, 600 pipes of wine ready wherewith they are returned to the fleet, and hired a merchantman to bring what themselves could not stow: In the meantime not knowing how far the whole proportion was to be depended on, we went on to buy up some at Lisbon and Faro where 'twas indifferent cheap, so that we are now plentifully supplied as to quantity, though that from the Madeiras be not so fit for this use in regard of its sweetness and when it comes to be made up in beverage must be mingled with good store of the other wine (which is hard and sharp) else will not keep....

Naseby at anchor in Cadiz Bay the last of July 1656.

Add. MSS. B.M. 9300, 338*.

5.15   Blake to Secretary Thurloe.

The three victuallers are now with us; the two first came in the nick of time, that we were going into this port for bread.   The John and Abigail arrived here last Thursday. We do use all possible diligence to clear them of their victuals, that we may go to sea; but the great anxiety is how we may be enabled to keep the sea for want of liquor.   This country is wholly drained of beverage wines.   We cannot make up above six weeks drink at most; and I am enforced to buy up a quantity of good drinking wine for a reserve, to be disposed of among the seamen in case of necessity, which is a bad but our only expedient at present. I have likewise sent to Porto, to buy what wines are to be got there.   The supply, which is offered us of 400 pipes from the Madeiras, is a remedy no better than the disease, for they cannot be expected probably in less than two months; and where they may then find us, or if they should come to us at sea, how we shall get out the wines, and how they must be converted into beverage for the use of the fleet, without going to port, is a riddle to those, who are of experience, though to others perhaps it may seem easy.   These inconveniences might have been prevented by sending two months or but six weeks before.   I wish that his Highness were thoroughly informed of these things, that a better course may be taken in the future for the supply of his fleet, and the carrying on of his service in these or any other remote parts.   *Dec. 8. 1656.*

Thurloe 5.691*.

5.16   Blake to the Admiralty Commissioners

I doubt there is not that consideration had in the state of the victualling that I would conceive would be requisite for such voyages as these. As that the Pursers should be forced to take a month's bread in money, although they had stowage for it in kind, which those that were fitted out in London say that they were, though I believe most of them were willing enough, being necessitous persons. And then that there is not allowance for defective victuals, whereas the peas and flour we have left is generally decayed as some of other victuals likewise are, neither had we any fruit to spend with the flour while it was tolerably good: all which besides the underhand compacts that are (as we have too much cause to suspect)....to the prejudice of seamen; but of the service also, especially where we are under so great an uncertainty of timely supplies....

Swiftsure of Cape Vincent 19th November 1656.
Add. MSS. B.M. 9300,349*.

\-

5.17   Order by the Rt Hon Robert Blake, George Monck, John Disbrow, and William Penn, Admirals and Generals of the fleet of the Commonwealth of England

For the future prevention of abuses, and those sad and lamentable events which have formerly and likewise lately happened by unresistable accidents of implacable fire to several vessels of the navy and others .... It is hereby strictly ordered as followeth,

That no person of or in the fleet presume (after the watch is set) to have or keep any candles lighted between decks or in any other part of this or any other vessel in service of the Commonwealth except such are necessary to be employed about the ship's use, and those to be carried in lanthorns only, and that none but such be used in hold of this or any other vessel under pain of severe punishment, and hereof the lieutenant, the master, his mates, the quarter-masters, boatswain and mates, with the yeoman of each vessel are to take special care, and the Marshall General, with his deputies (in their several stations) are to take the offenders into immediate custody until censure do pass,

That no tobacco be taken between the decks of this or any other vessel of war, or in hold, or in the cabins of the same, under pain as aforesaid, and that all those mentioned in the former articles have a vigilant eye thereunto, and do endeavour to bring all delinquents to condign censure.

That no strong water or other strong drinks be sold within board of this or any other vessel in the service, whereby mariners may be intoxicated and rendered incapable of, and refractory to, duty, besides manifold mischances and mischiefs ensuing thereupon, and the breach hereof to be under most severe censure and punishment.

That copies hereof be by the Judge Advocate delivered and dispersed through the several ships present, the same to be fastened in some convenient place, with the captain's name subscribed, whereby due notice may be taken of the premises.

Onboard the Swiftsure, 17 December 1653.

S.P. 18. 42. 80*.

5.18   Blake and Mountagu to the Admiralty Commissioners

... the danger you mention the Bristol to have been in doth not a little affect us. Some danger of fire happening likewise herein the Unicorn on Saturday last, by reason of defects in the floor of her Cask-room; but as prudently observed and quenched with little or no damage to the ship;...To take all probable ways that.... may prevent the accidents for time to come ..... we have under consideration some strict orders to be given in charge to the officers of each ship. And do conceive which is also Commissioner Willoughby's opinion that if you please to appoint 4 Masons to go in the fleet, with materials of brick and other necessities to repair any decays which may happen about the Cask-rooms and furnaces, it may contribute much hereunto.

The Naseby in Stokes Bay 4 March 1656.

R.C. Anderson MSS*.

5.19   Blake and Mountagu to the Protector

While we were writing the letter, that comes herewith to your Highness there rose a very great storm of wind from the East and S.E. which hindered the captains, who were divers of them on board to receive their orders for England, from returning to their own ships till this morning and put most of the fleet from their anchors, and those that were not (all but seven or eight) drove a great way. Divers merchantmen in harbour of Cadiz were likewise forced out to sea. About one of the clock the following night the Taunton came driving in that stress of

wind directly upon us, and we had begun to cut two of our best cables to get off her way, but it pleased God in very much mercy, that she let slip, and getting a sail open with much ado steered clear of us, else one or both of us in all likelihood had immediately gone to the bottom. We have lost many of our boats, as also cables and anchors, but hope to recover a good part of them. Some of those put to sea begin to appear again, though we doubt it will be some time before all come together, and that we shall, find divers of them in a shattered condition.... Naseby, at anchor before Cadiz, 3rd July 1656.
Thurloe 5. 178*.

5.20   Blake and Mountagu to Secretary Thurloe

Since our last to his Highness....we have had some time to view over our damage sustained in the late storm, and find it to be very great; many of the fleet having lost their boats, and most of their cables and anchors; in particular the Resolution hath spoiled two of her best anchors, one of about 56 pound weight being broken in two, and the other bent so 'tis useless....
                                                  Naseby in Cadiz Bay 8 July 1656.
Thurloe 5.195*.

5.21   Blake to the Admiralty Commissioners

I.... set sail with the Speaker, Tredagh, and Providence and on the 14th following met with the rest of the fleet off Cape Vincent, who were by the Easterly winds then blowing fresh put so far to seaward. The night before we came the Fairfax had her head and boltsprit carried quite away by the Foresight who in tacking fell foul of her and a little after the Speaker spent her main yard; lesser damage in topmasts, sails etc. we received more frequently having had tedious weather for the first fortnight we came off the Cape.
                                   Swiftsure off Cape Vincent the 19th of November 1656.
Add. MSS., B.M. 9300, 349*.

5.22   Blake to the Admiralty Commissioners

....The now wind I find will be very prejudicial to our men's health; a little that we have had from the shore having already cast divers of them into the flux....
                                   Swiftsure off Cape Vincent the 19th of November 1656.
Add. MSS., B.M. 9300, 349*.

5.23　Blake and Monck to the Admiralty Commissioners

....Our men fall sick very fast every day, having at present on board this ship upwards of eighty sick men and some of them very dangerously, which we hear if generally through the whole fleet alike proportionable to the number of men on board, so that we shall be constrained to send a considerable number unto Ipswich for their recovery, where there is room enough for them and good accommodation, as we understand by a letter from Doctor Whistler lately come to our hands, to whom we have writ that special care might be taken of them and suitable provision made for them according to their conditions....

Resolution off of Winterton, the 4th July, 1653.
S.P. 38. 7*.

5.24　Blake to the Admiralty Commissioners

....Our number of men besides are lessened by reason of death and sickness occasioned partly through the badness of victuals and the long continuance of poor men at sea; the Capt. of the Fairfax tells me in particular that they are forced to call up all their company upon the deck whenever they go to tack; and most of the other ships that have been out from the beginning are well nigh as bad to pass....

George in the offing of Cadiz 8th March 1657
Add. MSS., B.M. 9300, 648*.

5.25　Monck and Blake to the Bailiffs of Aldeburgh

The Parliament by their resolves in December last have amongst other things provided for seamen in their service that such of them as should be sent sick ashore at any time into any port or town should be taken care of by the magistrates of such place where they shall come, and there being several sick men now in the fleet of the Commonwealth under our command part whereof we have thought fit to send unto you: desiring you would take care of them that they may be so accommodated, cared for, and looked after as is requisite for men in their condition....

Resolution the 5 July, 1653.
Aldeburgh Corporation MSS. 119*.

5.26   Blake and Deane to the Council of State

....We are miserably torn and have many men slain and wounded, and therefore humbly desire provisions, Chirugeons, and all other things needful may be had for the wounded men on the Coast between Weymouth and the Downs, where we have been necessitated to land them....

Triumph near the Isle of Wight, 22nd February, 1653.

Marquis of Bath MSS*.

5.27   Blake to Penn

There being many hundreds of Dutch officers and seamen lately taken dispersed abroad in the fleet, and there also being great numbers of our seamen disposed into the Dutch men-of-war, whereof no perfect cognisance hath yet been taken: These are therefore to desire you forthwith to cause strict inquiry to be made into all the ships and vessels belonging to your squadron, to know what numbers of Dutch there be aboard the several ships, and how many English are taken out of them for the manning of the said men-of-war, and in what ships they be; and likewise how all the ships of your squadron be at present manned, to the end that an orderly and equal distribution may be made of the said Dutch officers and mariners which may be with the least disabling of the several respective ships of the fleet, and the best advantage to the whole.   This being a business of consequence and that requires haste, I desire you will use all possible diligence therein that so a speedy, just, and impartial account may be given of the same for attending the ends aforesaid.

Aboard the Resolution 15th July, 1652.

You are likewise desired to cause inquiry to be made for what wounded Dutch men are still aboard any of the ships of your squadron, as also what number of Dutch here be that are unfit for service, old men or boys.

The Duke of Portland's MSS, Navy Papers, 1640-1696, fol.157*.

5.28   Blake to the Navy Commissioners

At our being at Algiers it was resolved amongst the seamen throughout the fleet upon a question put to that purpose that they would contribute every man a dollar towards the ransom of certain Dutch Captives who hoping to gain their liberty swam from the shore to our ships, the money to be stopped upon their account for short allowance....

8 oct. 55.

S.P. 18. 101. 26*.

5.29   Blake to the Lord Protector

.... our condition is dark and sad, winter drawing on and like to be very miserable, our ships extreme foul, our victuals expiring, all stores failing, our men falling sick, through the badness of drink and eating their victuals boiled in salt water for two months space, the coming of a supply uncertain (we received not one word from the Commissioners of Admiralty and Navy by the last) and though it come timely, yet if beer come not with it, we shall be undone that way. We have no place or friend, our recruits here slow, and our mariners (which I most apprehend) apt to fall into discontents, through their long keeping abroad. Our only comfort is, that we have God to lean upon, although we walk in darkness, and see no light. I shall not trouble your Highness with any complaints of myself, of the indisposition of my body, or troubles of mind.....

Aboard the George, in Castcayes Road, 30 August 1655.

Thurloe 3.718*.

5.30   Blake to Mountagu

....The Swiftsure in which I was is so foul and unwealdy through the defects of her sheathing laid on her for the voyage of Jamaica that thought it needful to remove into the George....all the rest of our fleet are in a bad condition and not fit to be kept out to the difficulties and hazard of another winter. Besides there is a great want of men which cannot possibly be recruited here and no provision for sick and wounded with many other discouragements. But the goodness of the Lord towards us is never to be forgotten is far greater than all the discouragements of men notwithstanding the great Tempests of Wind that we have encountered without the Straights and within. We are altogether and behold one another's Face with comfort....

Off Lagos Bay the 9th of February 1657.

The Earl of Sandwich MSS. at Hinchingbrooke*.

Plate VI A seaman's rations

The weekly allocation for a seaman in Blake's navy was:

7 pounds of biscuit, 4 pounds of salt beef, 2 pounds of salt pork, 1 quart of dried peas, 3 pints of oatmeal, 6 ounces of butter, 12 ounces of cheese, 7 gallons of beer and "all the fish that could be caught at sea without any deduction from the rations".

A plentiful supply of fresh water was needed to soak the dried and salted food.

[Admiral Blake Museum]

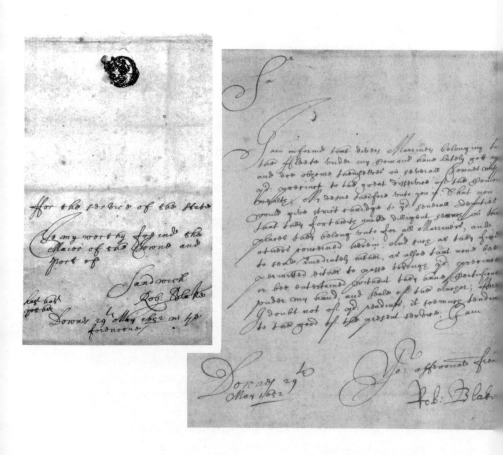

Plate VII Letter signed by Robert Blake

This letter dated 29th May 1652 (partly reproduced as 3.12) from Blake in the Downs to the Mayor of Sandwich asks for help in arresting deserters from the fleet. It bears the anchor seal of the Admiralty. Clearly the matter was urgent - the letter is marked "haste, haste, post haste". [Admiral Blake Museum]

CHAPTER 6 COMMUNICATIONS

Good communication was a fundamental pre-requisite for Blake and his fellow admirals' success, whether in the heat of battle or far from home in some distant Mediterranean station. A study of naval communication in the Interregnum shows it at an interesting formative stage.

Ships carried a variety of flags for **recognition**, to indicate nationality and the rank of the senior officers commanding in them - the origin of the term "flag officer" (**6.1 - 6.2**). Even the naval administration seems to have been confused by the precise conventions to be used (**6.3**). As the structure of command became more sophisticated, so communication needed to become more complex and flags began to be used for **signalling**, by flying different flags from different points of the ship. Initially this was to call officers on board the flagships for conferences (**6.4 and 6.5**), but it was extended to pass simple instructions through the fleet (**5.5**). A precise system of signalling by the firing of cannon at night and in fog was also beginning to develop (**6.5**). The convention at the beginning of the war was for conferences of senior officers and captains to determine strategy - which did not help an admiral such as Blake, impose direct authority on his captains. One of the problems was the lack of a complex signalling system - Blake could not issue complex orders at a distance. The *Fighting Instructions* and the *Sailing Instructions* of 1653 began to remedy this. Drumbeat and trumpet calls were used to summon men to duties on board the ships (**6.6**) and beacons were used in shore-to-ship communication (**6.7**).

When Blake was on his distant cruises in the Atlantic and Mediterranean for long periods the problems of communication were stretched to their limit. Blake invariably sent more than one copy of a letter by different ships, and where possible detailed reports needed to be delivered personally (**6.8 - 6.9**). As weeks stretched into months away, fresh instructions and replies to questions became increasingly urgent (**6.10**). Difficulties of communication were compounded by the fact that in both of Blake's last two voyages he was the recipient of secret orders from

Cromwell. Letters were often sent in cipher (**6.11 - 6.12**).

Trumpeters might carry routine messages (**6.13**), while trusted officers were used to convey confidential communications (**6.14**). When all else failed Prince Rupert instructed his captains to look for a message fixed to a pole on a remote island. In the event it was found and read by his pursuer, Robert Blake (**6.15**).

6.1   Blake's Warrant to Penn

Forasmuch as the Council of State have thought fit that you should command as Vice-Admiral of the fleet, these are therefore to authorise you forthwith to wear a flag on the foretop of the ship Triumph under your charge.

Dated this 21 May, 1652.

Duke of Portland MSS, Navy Papers, 1640-1696, folio 144*.

6.2   Blake and Deane to the Navy Commissioners

We have written twice unto you about flags, and Jacks for the ships of the fleet, and being now come down, find but one Standard, five 16 breadth flags, four eight breadth, and one ten breadth, we desire you in respect of our going to Sea in the first fair wind, that another Standard with the remainder of the flags, and Jacks ordered by the Council of State, may be speeded aboard the Triumph....
R.C. Anderson MSS.   *Tilbury Hope 19 April 1649.*

6.3   Blake and Deane to the Navy Commissioners

....Touching the flags etc. it seems strange you refer the proportions to be ascertained by us, yourselves knowing best the former allowances which we suppose are alike in number in every expedition, but since the issue depends upon our resolution we think it needful that you should make up what you have already sent for ourselves, to three standards for the Vice-Admiral and Rear-Admiral, with the Admiral Vice-Admiral and Rear-Admiral of Ireland three flags apiece, with two Jacks for every ship in the fleet. For the Ensigns and Pendants, you best know how many are wanting, which (whatsoever they are) with the flags that we desire may be no longer delayed.   *Lee Road, April 21.1649*.
S.P. 18. 1. 65*.

6.4 Instructions by Blake, Deane and Monck for the better ordering of the fleet in sailing, March 29 1653

5. As soon as the General puts abroad a flag in the mizen shrouds, and fires a gun, then all captains of the fleet are to repair on board the General, and if an ensign be put abroad in the same place, then all masters of ships are to repair on board as aforesaid; if the standard in the same place, then all the flag officers only are to repair on board the General; if a red flag the captains of the Admiral's squadron; if a white flag, the Vice-Admiral's and all the captains of his squadron; if a blue flag, the Rear-Admiral and all the captains of his squadron; if a standard on the ensign staff, the Vice- and Rear-Admiral of the fleet only; if a white flag on the ensign staff, then all the captains of the frigates that carry 30 guns and upwards; if a blue ensign on the ensign staff, than all captains of frigates both great and small; if the jack colours on the ensign staff the captains of ships that are not frigates.....

8. If anyone chance to see a ship or ships in the day time, more than our fleet, you are to put abroad your ensign, and there keep it till ours is out and then to strike it as many times as you see ships, and stand with them, that we may know which way they are and how many....

16.7 If it prove thick and foggy weather, and we have sea room enough, we shall haul in our sails and shoot every hour a piece of ordnance, which the flag officers of our own squadron are first to answer, secondly the Vice-Admiral with his flag officers, and thirdly the Rear-Admiral with his flag officers and all the fleet are each to answer by firing off guns, beating of drums and sounding of trumpets. If we chance to anchor in the night, or in a fog, we shall shoot off two pieces of ordnance, the Vice- and Rear-Admiral of our squadron are each to answer with one presently after, then the Vice-Admiral of the fleet two, Vice-Admiral and Rear-Admiral each one, then the Rear-Admiral of the fleet two, his Vice- and Rear-Admiral each one, where by the ships of each particular squadron may have timely notice, to the end they may anchor near their respective flags under which they are....

Duke of Portland MSS. Navy Papers 1640-1696 fol. 178*

6.5 Blake to Penn

I desire you to give notice to the commanders of your squadron that they repair on board this ship to-morrow morning by 7 or 8 of the clock, that we may together seek unto the Lord and consider what is further to be done. Likewise to give them notice that it should before that time prove foul weather, a rendezvous for the fleet in case of separation is, if the wind be northerly Southwold Bay, is southerly taken off the Spurn....

You are likewise to communicate the word, viz. Patience, Hope.

Resolution, 3 Aug. 1652.

The Duke of Portland's MSS, Navy Papers 1640 - 1696, fol.159*.

6.6 Blake and Popham to officers and constables

By virtue of a power given us as Admirals and Generals of the fleet we authorise you to impress for the service of the fleet now setting forth to sea such and so many Able Trumpeters as shall from time to time be found necessary and particularly a complete noise for the ship appointed for us giving them Conduct money for their repair to Chatham. And this shall be your warrant

Dated at Whitehall 10th January 1650.

S.P. 18. 6. 99*.

6.7 Blake to the Navy Commissioners

This is only to recommend unto your favour the desire of the bearer Mr Nicholas Whetstone, postmaster of Deal, who is going to attend you for the usual sum of four pounds allowed for making fires upon the beach to give notice to the ships when any packet comes....

Downes, 26 March 1652.

S.P. 18. 27. 59*.

6.8   Blake to the Lord Protector

Yesterday I sent away by the Merlin frigate a packet (of which there comes herewith a duplicate) giving your Highness an account of the proceedings and condition of the fleet under my command. Since that the Taunton frigate is arrived with Mr. Thomas Maynard, whom I have dispatched away in the Hampshire, to give your Highness an account of his negotiation. I have nothing to add of my own as touching that business, having not received any other instructions or direction, but to appoint the frigate to carry him to and from Lisbon; and upon her return to me, to send him forthwith unto your Highness, to give an account of what he hath done in pursuance of the instructions given him....

Aboard the George in Castcais Road, August 31, 1655.

Thurloe 3, 752*.

6.9   Blake to the Lord Protector

The packet sent by Lieu. Major, master of the smack, with the instructions of the 13 and 14 of June, and also another for sending some part of the fleet I received Monday last about midnight. The secret instructions concerning the plate fleet expected from, as also other ships bound to America shall be carefully observed as God gives opportunity. The twelfth of last month I sent your Highness an account of our affairs by Capt Peck in the Amity as also two duplicates by the Fame and Ketch which I hope are, or will shortly come to your Highness's hands; since which time there is not anything. That your Highness may have speedy notice of my receipt of your last commands, I have dispatched away this smack before intending in obedience to the same to send after a part of the fleet, as soon as all are come together, some being at present employed in fetching liquor.....

Aboard the George in the Bay of Lagos, July 4, 1655.

Thurloe 8, 611*.

6.10   Blake to the Admiralty Commissioners

....What supplies are intended us or the time and place we may in probability expect them we are as yet wholly ignorant of more than the guess I may make from the knowledge you have of our necessities. His Highness was pleased to refer to your letters for our particular advice intimating that you had direction to write at large therein and it would have been of great encouragement to the fleet (if complied with) whom we cannot keep from being sensible of the conditions they are left in, but I am apt to think some packet hath miscarried having received none from you since that by the Lark only inferior officers have letters of late date saying some of them that no victuals are designed us, others that those that were, are diverted for the West Indies and we expected home which they disperse among the seamen to my trouble: and I mention it that you may the better judge how convenient it is, we should have more frequent and particular advice from yourselves....

Swiftsure off Cape Vincent the 19th of November 1656.

Add. MSS., B.M. 9300, 349*.

6.11   Blake to Secretary Thurloe

I have received your letter of the 14th of June sent by the Endeavour smack, together with the inclosed cipher for which I thank you. Though I have carefully preserved the original, I cannot enlarge myself at present, according as I desire, being encumbered with accidental businesses, but shall give you further account of affairs by the ships which I am to send from the fleet.

Aboard the George off Lagos Bay, July 4. 1655.

Thurloe 3.611*.

6.12   Blake to the Lord Protector.

Secret instructions sent by your Highness referring me to a former instruction touching the silver fleet of Spain, coming from America, I have received and shall carefully observe the same.   We had information at Cadiz that the fleet was expected about a month or five weeks hence.   We are now off Cape Maries intending to spread with the fleet what we can and to range this sea according to the wind the information we can get plying over likewise towards Cape Sprat it being their most likely and usual course.

George, June 12, 1655.

Thurloe, 3.541*. (this letter is in a number cipher)

6.13   Messenger's expenses

The charges of Thomas Williams, Trumpeter, being employed by the Admirals of England; Col. Blake and Col. Popham by several times sent employed with letters to the King of Portugal.

[19 occasions are specified.]

Mr. Powell pray pay unto Thomas Williams being employed upon several messages as above specified the sum of five pounds, sixteen shillings.

6th. April 1650

S.P. 18. 12. 4.

6.14   Blake and Mountagu to Meadows, the English envoy at Lisbon

The bearer Lieutenant Morgan, being a person in whom we confide, understands something of our thoughts touching the business we would speak with you about; to whom you may give credit in anything he shall deliver.
Naseby in Cadiz-bay, 20th of May 1656.

Note here, That it being not thought expedient to mention the sailing of the fleet in the letter, lest it should be opened by the Portugals between Cascais and Lisbon, the lieutenant of the Naseby was ordered to communicate it by word of mouth, and to let Mr. Meadows know, he should no need to go beyond Cape-Pitcher, as the generals hoped to meet them.
Thurloe 5. 44*.

6.15 Blake to the Council of State

... I put to sea, and the 12th of Nov. came to an Anchor under the Isle of Forementera, the place appointed for their Rendezvous, as we understood Capt. Burley's instructions, Capt. of the Roebuck. There accordingly we found a paper in a box fastened to a staff, with a white flag on top, which I have herewith sent to your Honours. From thence we bent our course immediately towards Majorca, conceiving that might be the place meant in the paper; but finding no intelligence of them there, they having got the start of us so many days, as by the paper appeareth, and in all probability according to the winds, got either Villa Franca or Toulon.....

From aboard the Bonaventure in Cadiz Bay, 21st. Dec. 1650.

Weekly Intelligencer 17. E. 621*.

CHAPTER 7 INTO ACTION

Blake's accounts of his battles lack detail. Whether this was his natural modesty and reticence - he always attributed his victories to the intervention of the Almighty - or whether he knew others regularly wrote in more detail, we do not know. His accounts of the Battles of the Kentish Knock and Portland are so sketchy that they have to be reconstructed entirely from the reports of others. Nevertheless his relation of his two encounters with Rupert off Lisbon in August and September 1650 does re-create the essence of the actions (**7.1 and 7.2**). His terse story of the capture of the Frenchman (**7.3**) raises as many questions as it answers. The account of the storming of Jersey, 1651, (**7.4**) is interesting because it was a successful amphibious assault. Two battles from the Anglo-Dutch War feature here - Dover, May 1652, (**7.5**) and Dungeness, November 1652 (**7.6**). Blake's successful attack on Porto Farina (**7.7**) presaged his more illustrious assault on Santa Cruz, though for the latter we must rely on the accounts of Stayner and others for detail (**Appendix 5**).

7.1   Blake and Popham to the Council of State

.....*The 26th July between 9 and 10 in the morning Prince Rupert after long preparation and much noise came forth of the Bay of Weyres with 26 ships 18 Carvells, the wind at E.S.E. our fleet being then at anchor near Cascais Road we forthwith weighed and stood off with them, they keeping the wind of us. Having got a reasonable Berth from the shore we hauled our foresails to the Mast with our fleet which then consisted of 10 sail beside the Brazil ships our Cales squadron being not returned, The Hercules and Assurance off at sea, the Providence at Virgo for water and the Constant Warwick on her way from England. The enemy still kept the wind, the French Admiral with four fireships being the headmost of their fleet, and a stern of him about a mile from the Reformation. A little after the wind coming to the S. we filled our sails, tacked and got the wind which the Enemy perceiving tacked likewise, then we bore away large upon the Frenchman being betwixt us and the Reformation, and exchanged some shot with him, as also did the Phoenix. But as fast as we bore upon him he bore away large in towards the harbour, and Rup: likewise (his mizzen always hauled up). We followed them until we came into ten fathom water near the South Hetchoops and then it drawing toward night, having a lee shore, and a Leeward Tide and being in the Indraught of the harbour we submitted to the present necessity, and stood off the enemy coming to anchor between the two Castles...*

From aboard the Resolution riding off the Port of Lisbon, 15 August 1650.

Portland Papers. N.S.17*.

7.2   Blake to the Council of State.

....Four days after our parting, being Saturday, about eleven in the morning we discovered a part of Rupert's and the Portugal fleet in the mist, and about four in the afternoon, we found ourselves very near the whole fleet, consisting of 36 sail. I had only one with me the Phoenix and Expedition, having lost the rest in the fog. By God's good providence, the enemies' fleet was all to leeward of us, so we keeping the wind made toward them being resolved to encounter Prince Rupert, who was the headmost of the fleet. Coming within reach, we gave him a broadside, so did the two frigates, which the Lord was pleased so to Direct, that his foretopmast was shot off by the cap.Whereupon he bore up into the midst of the fleet and the thick mist taking them again out of our sight, we stood off to seek the rest of our squadron, which we met with the next day. The Saturday following early in the morning, we discovered the Brazil fleet bound for Lisbon consisting of 21 sail. I forthwith made toward the admiral, who being too nimble, I fell on the rearadmiral being a ship of no less force, and had above three hours' dispute with him, it blowing very much wind, so that we could not use our lower tier. At length after loss of many of his men, he yielded, we being so near that at going off, the head of our ship received a crack. We took in all seven prizes having in them above 4000 chests of sugar, and near 400 prisoners. The viceadmiral was burnt, being first boarded by the Assurance, who saved most of the remainder of his men. The wind being northerly and very much, our prizes torn and lame, and our liquor very near spent, I bore up for this place wither by God's blessing we came all in safety.

From aboard the George in the bay of Cadiz, October 14. 1650.

Portland MSS. at Welbeck Abbey. N. 17.96*.

7.3   Blake to the Council of State

The day after I had despatched away Captain Badiley with the George and other ships for England....I went aboard the Phoenix, and being at sea four or five leagues off the Straits' mouth met with a French man of war, who after some dispute yielded upon quarter. There was in her 36 brass guns, and 180 men, the Captain Chevalier de la Lande, commander of a squadron....

The Leopard in the Road of Malaga, 30th October, 1650.

Portland Papers N. 17. 96*.

Note : Popham's departure and subsequently Badiley's, left Blake with no serviceable "great ships". Transferring to the 4th Rate *Phoenix* (38 guns), a smaller ship than he would normally fly his flag in, he set out to prevent French help reaching Rupert and encountered the 36-gun French warship *Jules*. Five accounts of what happened differ on whether there actually was a fight, but there is a suggestion that the French were overawed by Blake and this led to the surrender of the *Jules*.

7.4   Blake to the Speaker of the House of Commons

It hath pleased God, that after much conflicting with sea and winds, and other difficulties, and a short dispute with the enemy: about 11 at night on Wednesday last, our force landed on the south[1] side of the Island in a bay called Portala Mar[2], with good resolution and success. The enemy after a hot charge with their horse flying before them, forsaking divers small Works and Forts; the next day our men took by surrender the tower of St. Albin, with 14 guns in it, which affordeth refuge and safety for our victualling ships and others. Cartaret is gone to Elizabeth Castle, which is blocked up by a party. The rest of our men are nowhere about the Fort of Mount Orgel, our ships riding before it. We have not lost above 4 or 5 men as far as I can learn; some Barques and other vessels are still in that Bay aground, and have received some damage since the landing, it hath been such weather, as I could not have intercourse with the shore, so that I cannot give your Honours a perfect narrative.

Aboard the Happy Entrance in the road of St. Katherine, 26 October. 1651.

Faithful Scout 42. E. 791*.

1   A slip of the pen - it was the west of the island.
2   Port de la Mer in St. Ouen's Bay.

69

7.5 Blake to the Speaker of the House of Commons

I have dispatched away the express to your Honours to give you an account of what passed yesterday between us and the Dutch fleet, being in Rye Bay. I received intelligence from Major Bourne that Van Tromp, with forty sail, was off the South Sand-head, whereupon I made all possible speed to ply up towards them, and yesterday, in the morning, we saw them at anchor in and near Dover Road. Being come within three leagues of them, they weighed and stood by a wind to the eastward, we suppose their intention was to leave us to avoid the dispute of the flag. About two hours after they altered their course and bore directly with us, Van Tromp the headmost; whereupon we lay by and put ourselves into a fighting posture, judging they had a resolution to engage. Being come within musket-shot I gave order to fire at his flag, which was done thrice. After the third shot he let fly a broadside at us. Major Bourne, with those ships that came from the Downs, being eight, was then making towards us. We continued fighting till night; then our ship being unable to sail by reason that all our rigging and sails were extremely shattered, our mizzen-mast shot off, we came with advice of the captains to an anchor about three or four leagues off the Ness, to refit our ship, at which we laboured all the night. This morning we espied the Dutch fleet about four leagues distance from ours towards the coast of France, and by the advice of a council of war it was resolved to ply to windward to keep the weather-gage, and we are now ready to let fall our anchor this tide. What course the Dutch fleet steers we do not well know, nor can we tell what harm we have done them, but we suppose one of them to be sunk, and another of thirty guns we have taken, with the captains of both. The main mast of the first being shot by the board, and much water in the hold made Captain Lawson's men to forsake her. We have six men of ours slain, and nine or ten desperately wounded, and twenty-five more not without danger; amongst them our master and one of his mates, and other officers. We have received above seventy great shot in our hull and masts, in our sail and rigging without number, being engaged with the whole body of the fleet for the space of four hours, and the mark at which they aimed. We must needs acknowledge a great mercy that we had no more harm, and our hope the righteous God will continue the same unto us if there do arise a war between us, they being first in the breach, and seeking an occasion to quarrel....

From aboard the James, 3 leagues off the Hydes, the 20th May, 1652.

Tanner MSS. 53. fol 35*.

7.6   Blake to the Admiralty Committee

I presume your Honours long for an account of what hath passed between us and the Dutch fleet, and I hope you have hearts prepared to receive evil as well as good from the hand of God. It pleased Him on Monday last, when we went out of the Downes (the wind at out weighing being S.W.) to raise a fresh gale, which was a while variable, but after blew strongly at N.W., so that we could not that day engage. The wind increased at night, we riding in Dover Road, and the enemy about two leagues to leeward of us at anchor. The next morn proving less wind (the enemy first weighing) we weighed and stood away, keeping the wind to the Ness to get clear of the Rip-raps before engagement, the enemy sailing fair by us. About the pitch of the Ness the headmost of our fleet met and engaged the enemy's fleet, consisting of 95 sail, most of them great ships; three admirals, two vice-admirals, and two rear-admirals. They passed many broadsides upon us very near, and yet we had but six men slain and ten wounded. About the same time the Victory was engaged with divers of the enemy, but was relieved by the Vanguard and some others. The Garland sped not so well, but being boarded by two of their flags and others, and seconded only by Captain Hoxton, was, after a hot fight board-and-board, carried by them, and his second with him. It was late before I took notice of it, whereupon I gave order to bear up to them, but immediately our foretopmast was shot away, our main-stay being shot before, and our rigging much torn, so that we could not work our ship to go to their relief; and by occasion thereof, and night coming on, we were saved ourselves, who were then left almost alone. As soon as it was night we made sail toward Dover Road and came to anchor.

Triumph in the Downes this 1st December 1652.

The Duke of Portland's MSS. Navy Papers, 1640-1696 fol.169*.

7.7   Blake to Secretary Thurloe

....After our arrival we found them more wilful and untractable than before, adding to their obstinacy much insolence and contumely, denying us all commerce of civility, and hindering all others as much as they could from the same. These barbarous provocations did so far work upon our spirits, that we judged necessary for the honour of the fleet, our nation, and religion, seeing they would not deal with us as friends, to make them feel us as enemies, and it was thereupon resolved at a Council of war, to endeavour the firing their ships in Porto Farina. The better to effect the same, we drew off again and sailed to Trapani (our occasional likewise agreeing thereunto) that so they might be the more secure. After the stay of some days there, we set sail back for Porto Farina, where we arrived the 3rd instant in the afternoon, and met again a Council of war, at which it was resolved by the permission of God, to put in execution our former intentions. Accordingly the next morning very early, we entered with the fleet into the harbour, and anchored before their castles, the Lord being pleased to favour us with a gentle gale off the sea, which cast all the smoke upon them, and made our work the more easy, for after some hours' dispute, we set on fire all their ships, which were in number nine, and the same favourable gale still continuing we retreated out again into the road. We had twenty five men slain and about forty hurt, with very little other loss. It is also remarkable by us that shortly after our getting forth, the wind and weather changed and continued very stormy for many days, so that we could not have effected the business, had not the Lord appointed that nick of time, in which it was done.....

Aboard the George in Calary Bay, the 18 April 1655.

Thurloe. 3. 390*.

CHAPTER 8 BLAKE THE MAN

Robert Blake's letters were primarily concerned with getting things done and the reader will have already formed an impression of the man from his actions. Such was his natural reticence and modesty, it is only occasionally that Blake refers to his personal circumstances, but the collected extracts in this chapter do provide some of the brushwork to the picture of the man.

Blake was well into middle age when he was appointed to naval command and he clearly relished his life at sea. In the Autumn of 1649 he was offered a prestigious military command in Ireland (**8.1**) and he is at pains to solicit the help of his friend and fellow general Popham to find a polite way of refusing.

His commitment to the cause of the Commonwealth was only surpassed by a real desire to bring Prince Rupert to book and he betrays real frustration that he had to leave the final pursuit to others (**8.2**).

Blake expected his captains to show determination equal to his. This did not always happen and he complains bitterly that he was not given support at the Battle of Dungeness (**8.3**). This letter shows a rare instance of Blake's confidence being dented. He begs to be allowed to lay down his command, which up to that point in the Dutch War he had held alone, as Parliament had mobilised Deane and Monck ("two such able gentlemen"), the other two Generals at Sea.

Though they saw themselves as instruments of the Almighty in a just war (**8.4**), Blake and his fellow commanders abhorred the human cost of the Dutch War. They did all they could to see that widows and orphans received support (**8.5**) - though there was also a practical reason for their concern.

It was partly as a result of his wound at the Battle of Portland that Blake's health began to fail. In his letter of 2nd June 1653 (**8.6**) we find Blake, still not fully fit, hastening to gather a squadron to support Deane and Monck, which he subsequently did at the Battle of the Gabbard. Though they looked forward to the end of the quarrel with England's Protestant neighbour, Blake and his colleagues remained vigilant to the end of the war (**8.7**).

Blake's letter to the Admiralty Commissioners before he set out on his second Mediterranean cruise (**8.8**) is interesting on a number of counts. It shows that it was not just the ordinary seamen's pay that was months in arrears. It is clear that Blake knew his health was failing. Though there are frequent references to his religious faith, this letter is unique in that it gives a clear statement of his Protestant creed.

This deep religious faith shows clearly in the letter that followed a week later (**8.9**). God's will, expressed through adverse winds, could dictate the sailing of the fleet and this had to be accepted. However worldly powers were to be thanked for worldly favours - Blake's brother Benjamin had been appointed to command the *Gloucester* in Penn's expedition to the West Indies.

Politics and religion combine in **8.10**. Shows of loyalty to the government and religious observance were important for morale, but Blake seems to have had a genuine desire to see a return to constitutional parliamentary rule, even though he had little faith in the selfishness and factions of those who sat in Parliament (**8.11**).

Blake's letter to Thurloe after the victory at Porto Farina (**8.12**) shows Blake using the Almighty to justify his political actions - an interesting conflict of conscience on the part of a commander far from home and lacking precise instructions, who was all too conscious of both the power of God and of Mammon. He argues that, though he had no direct orders to attack, the window of good weather which made the fleet's success possible, must indicate God's approval of the enterprise. This his earthly master Cromwell should (and did) respect. The months at sea wore on and conditions became worse and Blake, who by now was racked by disease and pain, became depressed, yet still the old man's faith in his Maker never wavered (**6.29**).

As his life drew to a close and he embarked on his last voyage, Blake seems to have been more open in his letters and conversation to those amongst the new political establishment that he could trust - specifically Thurloe and Mountagu (**8.13 and 8.14**). By October 1656, as he faced yet another winter at sea without the support of his new young colleague who had been ordered home to England, Blake was entering the darkest period of his life. Yet he still showed a real care for the search for a political and constitutional settlement at home and was still mindful of the Royalist threat ("our old enemies at home and their complices in Flanders")(**8.15**).
He was still able to write words of kindness to Mountagu, even though his own physical condition was worsening (**8.16**). Both the last comment in this letter and that to the Admiralty Commissioners a month later **8.17**) - show Blake knew he had not long to live, but he continued to pray to his God for the strength for one more campaign. His prayers were answered, for his last and greatest victory was still to come

8.1   Blake to Popham

I have received a letter from the Lord Lieutenant of Ireland, inviting me with much affection to be Major-General of his foot and telling me that he had written to some friends in London to obtain it. It was a strange surprise - greater than that of my present employment, which although it was extremely beyond my expectations as well as merits I was soon able to resolve upon by your counsel and friendship. This resolution remains the same and I pray you that if the motion be not yet made public you will interpose your interest for the prevention of it or to, oppose it if it shall be, that I may not be brought to that great unhappiness as to waive any resolution of Parliament, which in this case I shall be constrained to do........I desire from my heart to serve the Parliament in anything I can, so I shall account it in an especial happiness to be able to serve them in that conjunction which they have already placed me. If they please otherwise to resolve I shall content with a great deal more cheerfulness to lay down the command than I took it up, and in private to contribute the devoutest performance of my soul for their humour and prosperity.

1649, September 16. Aboard the Lion off the Old Head[1].
Leyborne Popham MSS*.

1   The Old Head of Kinsale, S.E. Ireland

8.2   Blake to the Council of State

Since my last to your honours of the 30 of October last from Malaga road by the Hopewel Ketch, it hath pleased God to deliver into our hands, and to destroy a great part of Prince Rupert's fleet.....I should have accounted it my greatest outward happiness if in recompense for all the charge this Commonwealth hath been at, I could have put a final conclusion thereto by the total destruction of that Piratical crew, but the will of God being otherwise I must acquiesce in it; and so I trust your Honours will be pleased to afford your favourable construction upon the endeavours of him who desires no greater worldly happiness, than to be accounted honest and faithful in this employment, and in it.

From aboard the Bonaventure in Cadiz Bay, 21st. Dec. 1650.
Weekly Intelligencer 17. E. 621*.

Plate VIII Robert Blake's sea chest
Acquired from the United Services Museum, this is one of the most prized possessions of the Admiral Blake Museum. Of mid 17th Century Spanish manufacture, the leatherwork facing was added at a later period. It is tempting to believe that many of the letters were written, or signed, on this.

[Admiral Blake Museum]

77

Numb. 375'

Mercurius Politicus,

COMPRISING

The fum of Forein Intelligence, with
the Affairs now on foot in the three Nations

OF

ENGLAND, SCOTLAND, & IRELAND;

For Information of the People,

—— Ità vertere Seria {Horat. de
{Ar. Poet.

From Thursday August 6. to Thursday August 13. 1657.

From Cadiz in Spain July 14.

Aptain *Vincart* of *Zealand* went lately with
two ships from hence to the *Canaries*;
the *English* had them in examination fix
houres long : moft of the *English* ships are
gone from this Road, becaufe their fleet
went out to Sea for fome days. The ship
called the *Flying Fame*, Skipper *Matthew
Hoock*, coming hitherwards from the *Canaries*, was purfued by
4 *English* Frigats, and the faid ship ftranded near *Guelva*, but
the *English* fetcht her off with the flood ; many Spanifh paf-
sengers

33 L

Whitehal, August 10.

Laft night came news, that fome of our Ships, more foul
then the reft, were returning home, together with General
Blake himfelf, from the Coaft of Spain , he being fick nigh
unto death

This morning came the unwelcome news of the death of
that gallant General ; a man of great honor, that had wholly
devoted himfelf to the fervice of his Country, and who gave
many proofs of an extraordinary courage and conduct, in actions both by Sea and Land. He hath been along time decay-
ing, and in his return being come to the Lizzard Point, finding himfelt to fail, he called feveral of the Commanders of
the other fhips aboard his own, to confer with them ; afterwards, drawing on towards his laft, he willed them to bear up
with all fpeed for Plimouth, hoping to have reached Land before his death ; but in the very entrance into the Sound of
Plimouth he expired. His body being imbowelled, and clofed
in a fheet of Lead, the Bowels were interred there in the Ca-
thedral Church, and his Corps were fent along with the ships
toward the Downs. The fleet remains ftill upon the Spanifh
coaft.

Aug. 11. This day we had an account alfo touching the
death of Vice Admiral *Badiley*, who hath been fome time ab-
fent from Sea, by reafon of indifpofition of Body; and of
late, going to the Waters in hope of recovering health, he
decayed more and more, and hath exchanged this life for a
better.

Aug. 12. Intelligence was brought, that the ships which
arived lately at Plimouth, were come into the Downs to Gen.
Mountague, and had brought the Corps of Gen. *Blake* thither.
Alfo, that the ship lately taken as fhe returned from the Canaries, with the Spanifh Officers, hath aboard her in Plate, &c. to
the value of about 80000 l, and alfo the faid Officers.

This week alfo arived in the Downs, an Ambaffador Extraordinary from the King of Portugal, by name Don *Francifco
de Mello*, General of the Artillery in that Kingdom, who is
come fince to Graves-end, and from thence he fhortly cometh
to London.

London, Printed by *Tho Newcomb* dwelling in *Thames ftreet over
against Bainards Cafle.*

Plate IX Newspaper announcing Blake's death
Mercurius Politicus appeared weekly throughout the Commonwealth period.
This edition reads: "This morning came the unwelcome news of that gallant
General; a man of great honor, that had wholly devoted himself to the service of
his Country, and who gave many proofs of an extraordinary courage and
conduct, in actions both by sea and land." It also records the death of one of
Blake's regular shipmates, Vice Admiral Badiley.

[Admiral Blake Museum]

8.3   Blake to the Admiralty Committee

....*In this account I am bound to let your Honours know in general that there was much baseness of spirit, not among the merchant-men only, but many of the State's ships, and therefore I make it my humble request that your Honours would be pleased to send down some gentlemen to take an impartial and strict examination of the deportment of several commanders, that you may know who are to be confided in and who are not.....And I hope it will not be unseasonable for me, in behalf of myself, to desire your Honours that you would be pleased to think of giving me, your unworthy servant, a discharge from this employment, so far too great for me; especially since your Honours have added two such able gentlemen for the undertaking of that charge; so that I may spend the remainder of my days in private retirement and in prayers to the Lord for a blessing upon you and for the nation......At the close of this I received your Honours' of the 30th November, together with your commission, which I shall endeavour to put in execution with all the power and faithfulness I can, until it shall please your Honours to receive it back again, which I trust will be very speedily, so that I may be freed from that trouble of spirit which lies upon me, arising from the sense of my own insufficiency and the usual effects thereof, reproach and contempt of men, and the disservice of the Commonwealth, which may be the consequence of both. Into what capacity or condition soever it shall please the Lord to cast me, I shall labour still to approve myself a faithful patriot....*

Triumph in the Downes this 1st December 1652.

The Duke of Portland's MSS, Navy Papers, 1640-1696, fol.169*.

8.4   Blake, Deane and Monck to the Speaker of the House of Commons

....*Thus you see how it hath pleased the Lord to deal with us poor unworthy instruments employed in this late transaction.....We have ma(n)y men wounded, and divers both of honesty and worth slain.   The condition of the widows and orphans of the ones, as also the languishing estate of the other, we do humbly present to your consideration, and most earnestly desire that you will be pleased to take such effectual course for the relief and supply of them, as may be answerable to the great trust God hath reposed in you, and His mercy bestowed upon you and this nation, and as may encourage others of faithfulness and honesty (if there shall be further cause) to hazard their lives and limbs in the future for the preservation and interest of God's people, those rights and liberties which God and nature hath afforded us.....*

Aboard the Triumph the 27 Feb., 1653, in Stokes Bay.

Tanner MSS 53 fol 215*.

8.5   Blake and Monck to the Admiralty Commissioners

Upon the 19th present some of frigates....met with eleven sail which proved to be Dutch ships....and being ships of force they fought for some time....In this encounter Capt. Vesey, commander of the Martin, was slain whom we understand hath left a poor widow with a great charge of children whose condition we leave to your consideration....

Resolution plying between the Texel and the Vlie 28th June 1653 at 6 in the evening.

S.P. 37. 73*.

8.6   Blake to the Navy Commissioners

.....being desirous to put in for my share for the service of the Commonwealth in this present juncture. If it please God to call us thereunto in any short time, such as the infirmity of my body will bear, which I find increases upon me.

Aboard the Essex middle of the Gunfleet 2nd June 1653.

S.P. 37. 8*.

8.7   Blake and Penn to the Admiralty Commissioners

...We are sorry to hear that the treaty between the Dutch and this Commonwealth is come to no certain resolution, their delay portends no great hopes of agreement, the consideration whereof doth quicken our former endeavours that such of the fleet now here may be ready for service upon all commands, and so hope the like with you.

Swiftsure at the Spithead, 4 Feb, 1654.

S.P. 18. 66. 9*.

8.8   Blake to the Admiralty Commissioners

These few lines are to desire that you will be pleased to give order unto the Commissioners of the Navy at Tower Hill to make a bill for the payment of my salary unto the day of the date hereof, it being uncertain whether I may live to see you again another. However, my comfort is, and I doubt not but, we shall meet together at the last day in the joyful fruition of that One faith and hope of the common salvation in the Lord, upon whom alone I do wait and to whose free grace and everlasting goodness I do heartily recommend you....

Plymouth, the 25th. of Aug: 1654

Add. MSS.B.M. 9304. F 89*.

8.9   Blake to the Admiralty and Navy Commissioners

...... The wind is now westerly and have been so ever since Wednesday, which was the day I limited, by my last unto you, for my putting to sea; which I cannot but pass without observing a hand of Providence therein, we are now doubly necessitated to wait upon the same; the Lord makes us to improve this necessity unto Christian virtue, not doubting but he will return all things to us for the best, if we can possess ourselves with patience and resign our wills to him that worketh all things at his good pleasure. I give thanks for your favours to my brother in answer to my letters which he delivered you, and not to trouble you with anything more at present...

Aboard the George in Plymouth Sound, 1 September 1654.

Addit MSS 9304. 91*.

8.10   Blake to the Admiralty Commissioners

Upon information that the 13th of this month is set apart to seek unto the Lord for a blessing upon the Parliament.   I have ordered the same to be observed throughout the Squadron that we may cast in our might into the Treasury of Prayer which will thus be put up unto and I hope accepted by the Lord......

George in Plymouth Sound, 8th, of September 1654.

Addit. MSS. 9304. 93.4*.

8.11   Blake to Secretary Thurloe

*Yours of the 25th January, as also the former mentioned in that, I have received.
In the latter you inform me of the dissolution of the Parliament, with the grounds
and consequences of it. I was not much surprised with the intelligence; the slow
proceedings and awkward motions of that assembly giving great cause to suspect
it would come to some such period; and I cannot but exceedingly wonder, that
there should yet remain so strong a spirit of prejudice and animosity in the minds
of men, who profess themselves most affectionate patriots, as to postpone the
necessary ways and means for preservation of the commonwealth, especially in
such a time of*
*concurrence of the mischievous plots and designs both of old and new enemies,
tending all to the destruction of the same. But blessed be the Lord, who hath
hitherto delivered, doth still deliver us; and I trust will continue so to do, although
he be very much tempted by us......*

Aboard the George in the bay of Calarie, March 14, 1655.

Thurloe 3.232*.

8.12   Blake to Secretary Thurloe

*.....It is also remarkable by us that shortly after our getting forth, the wind and
weather changed and continued very stormy for many days, so that we could not
have effected the business, had not the Lord appointed that nick of time, in which
it was done. And now, seeing it hath pleased God so signally to justify us therein,
I hope his Highness will not be offended at it, nor any who regard duels the
honour of our nation, although I expect to hear of many complaints and clamours
of interested men. I confess, that in contemplation thereof, and some seeming
ambiguity in my instructions (of which I gave you a hint in my last -) I did awhile
much hesitate myself, and was balanced in my thoughts, until the barbarous
carriage of those pirates did turn the scale.......*

Aboard the George in Calary Bay, the 18 April 1655.

Thurloe. 3. 390*.

8.13   Blake to Secretary Thurloe

I do cordially respect your mindfulness of me and of our affairs abroad expressed in divers letters particular in that of 13th June; for which I owe you many thanks and am glad of the occasion thereby given me to vent (though in a few lines) my troubled thoughts in our obscure condition which is likely to be more and more difficult every day....

April 1656.

Rawlinson A. 39.195. Thurloe 5.174.

8.14   Blake to Mountagu

I did very much sympathise with you in the stormy and contrary weather which I suppose you had shortly after our parting.   But I trust the Lord was with you in it and that this will find you safe and well in England.   Nor was I (though in a good Road) without my particular trouble and tossings.   This place is a prison to me....   What difficulties we are likely to encounter besides those which are ordinary to the season of the year and how hard a thing it will be to keep the whole squadron entire together to attend all opportunities of service for many reasons yourself can very well judge ....

Aboard the Swiftsure in the Bay of Weyers, Oct:10 1656.

Earl of Sandwich MSS at Hinchingbroke*

8.15   Blake to Secretary Thurloe.

Yours of the 4th November by the packet boat came to my hand the 5th instant. The welcome tidings of a right understanding between his Highness and the Parliament, the success of our friends abroad, more especially the timely check given by God's providence unto the proud hopes of our old enemies at home, and their complices in Flanders, hath not a little revived our sad spirits in the midst of so many difficulties here.

Dec. 8. 1656.

Thurloe 5.691*.

8.16   Blake to Mountagu

I wish you much good and firmness of strength by your retirement to Hinchingbrooke from hence the last two letters I received from you were dated the one the 13 and the other the 15 of Dec. As for us that are abroad the Lord hath been pleased in great mercy to provide for our safety and in particular for myself in supporting me against the many indispositions of my body so that by his blessing I doubt not to be enabled to continue out in the service the ensuing summer.....

Off Lagos Bay the 9th of February 1657.

The Earl of Sandwich MSS. at Hinchingbrooke*.

8.17   Blake to the Admiralty Commissioners

....I will not at present trouble you with any complaints of my particular infirmities the condition of my body growing every day weaker and weaker but I hope the Lord will support me till the appointed time; and trust likewise still continue gracious unto us, for the preservation of this fleet, for we have no confidence but in Him....

George in the offing of Cadiz 11th March 1657

Add. MSS., B.M. 9300, 648*.

APPENDIX 1 THE STRUCTURE OF COMMAND

Until the reforms of the Interregnum both the political and operational control of the Navy had usually been in the hands of the Lord High Admiral, latterly the Earl of Warwick. By 1649 the routine administration of the Navy was dealt with by the Navy Commissioners, and this did not change throughout the period. Operational command was often delegated to a working Vice Admiral. There was no regular establishment of subordinate flag officers. Men were nominated as needed as Vice Admirals and Rear Admirals to provide a chain of command purely for the duration of a particular cruise. Indeed at the beginning of this period the terms "Admiral", "Vice Admiral" and "Rear Admiral" indicate a function rather than a rank and are often used to refer to the leading ships of a fleet. The next substantive permanent rank was that of **Captain** and in the early part of the Interregnum Vice and Rear Admirals are regularly given the title "Captain" (**3.1, 9.4**). Such men would also be in direct charge of their own ship - they would not have a "flag captain".

In February 1649 after Warwick's dismissal, command of the navy was put in commission, i.e. it was to be shared. Popham, Blake and Deane (in that order of precedence) were appointed Generals at Sea (sometimes referred to at the time as Generals of the Fleet). The use of the term "general" for a naval commander was not new - Francis Drake while at sea was often referred to as "the general". More significantly, at the time, army officers were paid more than naval officers, and were reckoned to be senior. Thus in the early days of the Interregnum Blake and his fellows were usually addressed by their **army** rank e.g. "Colonel Blake, General at Sea". Blake's Rear Admiral at the Battle of Dungeness was always addressed by his army title - Major Bourne. Blake was offered the post of Major General in Ireland in late 1649 and regarded it as promotion - certainly the pay was greater - hence his embarrassment at turning it down (**8.1**). Only the commander of a fleet at sea (often referred to as "the general" whether he was technically one or not) had a flag captain to manage his ship and Blake sometimes shifted his flag from one ship to another.

The Generals at Sea only held **operational** command. The political power of the Lord High Admiral passed to the Council of State, in the early years of the Commonwealth, and operated through an ad hoc **Admiralty Committee** of which Sir Henry Vane the Younger, Treasurer of the Navy, was a leading member. Though the Generals at Sea might propose, it was the Committee and the Council that disposed.

The stresses of the First Anglo-Dutch War were to begin a process of change. It was acknowledged that the Council of State could not provide detailed supervision for the Navy. After the Battle of Dungeness a permanent **Admiralty Commission** was set up on which the Generals at Sea were ex officio members. One General at Sea - John Disbrowe, who never went to sea - was appointed specifically to help re-organise the Navy's administration.

At sea there were to be three regular squadrons - Red, White and Blue. According to the **Fighting Instructions** the Red Squadron would be commanded by two Generals (on the same ship), the White Squadron would be commanded by the Vice Admiral of the Fleet and the Blue Squadron by the Rear Admiral of the Fleet. Each squadron would have Vice and Rear Admirals in acting capacities - thus there would be ten flag officers. In effect this meant that the posts of Vice Admiral and Rear Admiral of the Fleet became substantive, and by the end of the Interregnum these ranks became used as regular titles.

APPENDIX 2 THE RATING OF SHIPS

By the time of the Civil War English naval ships had come to be classified in six rates (**A2.1**). The pay of the captain and officers was dependent on the rating, as was the allocation of petty officers (**A2.2**). The larger ships carried heavier guns and the rating of the ships reflected this. However the precise criteria for rating varied from time to time.

The largest ships, 1st and 2nd rates, were usually termed **"great ships"**. They were expected to be in the thick of large fleet actions - the progenitors of the later "ships of the line". By the Cromwellian period a **First Rate** would have three full gun decks with about 80 or more guns, the largest being cannon drakes (42 pounders). There were only three 1st rates in Blake's time, the *Resolution* (formerly *Prince Royal*) built in 1610, the *Sovereign* (formerly *Sovereign of the Seas*) built in 1637, and the *Naseby*, built in 1654. The *Sovereign*, the biggest warship in Europe, spent much of her time out of commission. A fourth First Rate, the *Richard*, was launched in 1658. Most of the **Second Rates** of the time were built in the reigns of Queen Elizabeth or King James I and these had two full gun decks and a third partial gun deck, though newer Second Rates had three gun decks. Usually they mounted 60-70 guns up to demi-cannon (32 pounders). During the Commonwealth large numbers of **Third Rate** ships were built. These carried most of the heavy guns of the Second Rates on two gun decks, and are often referred to as frigates. Usually they mounted 50-60 cannon including demi-cannon. These were considered more suitable for the needs of the navy than the larger, slower Second Rates. Flag officers would normally fly their flag in a "great ship".

Faster and more manoeuvrable were the **"frigates"**. They were often hired merchantmen or rented privateers, used for scouting and protecting convoys. beginning of the Commonwealth. It was the large privateer *Constant Warwick* which was used as the design for a new **Fourth Rate** frigate which was built in large numbers during the Interregnum. Flush decked, with around 40 guns (up to 18 pound culverins) on two gun decks these ships were fast but relatively powerful. In addition to traditional scouting and convoy duties they were used to deadly effect by Stayner and others as raiders and were large enough to be used in fleet actions. They played a significant role at Porto Farina and Santa Cruz. The Navy continued to employ smaller **Fifth Rate** frigates (around 20-30 guns), and utilised many captured prizes in this role. This class of ship carried demi-culverin (9 pounders). **Sixth Rates** were generally small ships used for scouting, as couriers and tenders. Usually they mounted less than a dozen of the smallest guns, 5 pounder sakers.

A2.1 (Copy manuscript in the Admiral Blake Museum)
August 3rd 1654; By the Commissioners for the Admiralty andNavie an Establishment of the Rates of the Ships of Warre belonging to Fleet of the Commonwealth of England

First Rate	Fourth Rate	Fifth Rate	Fifth Rate
Soveraigne	Winsby	Pearle	Mary Prize
Resolution	Ruuby	Nightingale	Old Warwicke
Naisby	Centurion	Mearmayde	Paul
3	Dyamond	Pembroke	Plover
Second Rate	Maydston	Faggons	Recovery
Triumph	Preston	Islip	Satisfaction
James	Nantwich	Grantham	Sorlings
George	Gaynsbrough	Selby	Union
Andrew	Taunton	Colchester	Wildman
Swiftsure	Jersey	Bazing	Greyhound
Raynebowe	Dover	Halfemoone	Mary Flyboat
Victory	Advice	Gilliflower	11
Paragon	Reserve	Rosebush	**Sixth Rate**
Vauntgard	Assistance	Falcon Flyboat	Nonesuch Ketch
Unicorne	Pellican	Adam and Eve	Catt Prize
10	Foresight	Westergate	Deptford Shallop
Third Rate	Great President	Sampson	Horsleydowne Shallop
Fairfax	Saphire	Golden Cocke	Henrietta Pinnace
Lyme	Portsmouth	Arms of Holland	Hopewell
Speaker	Phoenix	Tulip	Hare Ketch
Langport	Tyger	Cardiffe	Mayflower
Marston Moore	Elizabeth	Pellican Prize	Nichodemus
Torrington	Dragon	Falcon Fireship	Paradox
Plymouth	Nonsuch	Little Charity	Sparrowe
Bridgewater	Success	Falmouth	Truelove
Gloucester	Adventure	Hound	Weymouth
Tredagh	Assurance	Sun Prize	Wren
Newbery	Guinea	Dolphin	Martin
Worcester	Amity	Hector	Merlin
Essex	Expedition	Sophia	Drake
Lyon	Providence	Hope	17
Entrance	Constant Warwick	Advantage	
Indian	Great Charity	Augustine	
Mathias	Heartsease	Bryer	
17	Discovery	Crow	
Fourth Rate	Convertine	Convert	
Bristoll	Hampshire	Gift	
Newcastle	Princess Maria	Little President	
Laurell	Elias	Lizard	
Portland	Bear	Marmaduke	
Kentish	Welcome	Fox	
Yarmouth	41	Marigold	
6		Middlebouge 43	148 ships

89

A2.2 (Copy manuscript in the Admiral Blake Museum)
2nd September 1654
The number of Officers allowed on the States Ships

Rate	1st Rate	2nd Rate	3rd Rate	4th Rate	5th Rate	6th
Mates and Pilotts	6	4	3	2	2	1
Midshipmen	8	6	4	3	2	1
Boatswains Mates	2	2	1	1	1	0
Quarter Masters	4	4	4	4	3	2
Quarter Masters Mates	4	4	2	2	1	1
Carpenters Mates	2	<	manuscript damaged			>
Gunners Mates	2	2	2	1	1	1
Quarter Gunners	4	4	4	4	1	0
Chirugeons Mates	2	1	1	1	1	0
Ordinary Trumpeters	4	3	0	0	0	0

The number of Officers allowed in a
victualler ship 27th July 1654

Captayne

Master

Masters Mates one

Carpenter

Midshipmen

Carpenters Mate one

Carpenters Crew Four

Steward[1]

    8

His mate one

Cooke & mate one

    3

Cooper

& mates two

    3

Cheque[1]

The number of midshipmen allowed
on board the Ships of Generall
Penn's Squadron 20th August 1654

	Rank	
Ships of the	2	16
	3	12
		4
	5	6
	6	

Each Victuall ship

---

1   In 1653 in an effort to keep a check on the corruption rife amongst Pursers the duties of the post were split between the Steward and the Clerk of the Cheque, the theory being that each would monitor the other. The experiment did not work and was soon abandoned.

APPENDIX 3 NAVIGATION

Blake had no skill in navigation, though many of his captains were professional seamen. In any event all ships had a skilled sailing master who navigated the ship and it was the master and the pilot, not the captain, who would be held responsible if a ship ran aground. Masters were appointed because of their previous experience of the coasts that were the destination of the voyage. In the English Channel and North Sea, particularly during the Dutch War, the English navy relied heavily on the local knowledge of pilots, particularly since the Dutch used the shoals and sandbanks to shelter their fleets. We find Blake recruiting large numbers of pilots in 1652 in anticipation of hostilities **(A3.1 and A3.2)** and the pilots of Deal were able to prevail on Blake's favour in 1656 **(A3.3)**.

The science of navigation was at a transitional stage of development at the time. The magnetic compass had been used since the Middle Ages and the angles of the stars could be measured using a cross staff or sighting dial. Such measurement allowed latitude to be calculated. What was not available to Blake's navigators was any accurate measurement of longitude. Isaac Newton was to set out the principles of calculating longitude after the Restoration. But it was only when the Meridian of Greenwich came to be accepted as standard in the middle of the 18th Century, and an accurate marine chronometer was available that navigators could calculate longitude at sea and thus their precise position. (The first such chronometer was designed by Harrison and used by Captain Cook in 1772.)

The marine charts of the time reflected the state of knowledge then current. The Dutch cartographers were pre-eminent - both the Dutch East India and West India Companies had their own hydrographic offices and Dutch maps, or copies of them, were extensively used by English sailing masters. Mercator's projection (which took account of the curvature of the earth) had finally achieved general acceptance, and good charts showed compass bearings and lines of latitude as well as a fairly accurate outline of the coastline with the names of capes, bays, ports, islands etc. Sometimes charts included early sailing directions, sketches of local landmarks and, very exceptionally, details of the soundings and hazards to navigation in particular harbours. Such collections of charts were properly called "pilots" but were more popularly known as "waggoners" after the Dutch cartographer Lucas Waghenaer. However it was not until late in the reign of Charles II that Greenville Collins was commissioned to make detailed hydrographic surveys of the British coastline and not until 1795 that Alexander Dalrymple was commissioned to catalogue and systematise all the information collected by the Admiralty.

A3.1   Blake to the Mayor of Sandwich

Not knowing how soon there may be occasion for the fleet to put to sea; It is thought requisite for the advancement of the present service that you lay a strict command on all pilots experienced on the coast of Flanders and elsewhere not to stir abroad,but to attend till we shall send for them....

Downs 29th May 1652.

Sandwich Corporation MSS.*

A3.2   Blake to the Master, Wardens and Brethren of Trinity House, Dover

I formerly wrote to unto you about having in readiness all the Pilots that could be got in Dover and thereabouts, which I doubt but you have taken care in, but fearing the number by you provided should fall short of what the fleet requireth I therefore desire you to send forthwith to Ramsgate and all other places wherein any persons knowing the Coast of Flanders Holland, &c, do inhabit, commanding them to repair immediately hither as they will answer the contrary....

Dover Road, 20th June 1652.

Sandwich Corporation MSS.*

A3.3   Blake and Mountagu to Lord Lawrence, President of the Council

Whilst we rode an anchor in the Downs, divers of the Pilots of Deal....have made application to us, for our help, that their houses which they had built upon the beach at Deal might not be taken from them....and conceiving in our opinion that there is much reason and equity to have the same continued, and in regard the fleet do often resort to the place, and receive necessary assistance from the petitioners, we have presumed to send unto your Lordship their address unto us.... laying before your prudent consideration for such courses to be taken therein, as to your Lordship and the Council shall seem meet....

Aboard the Naseby in Stokes Bay, Feb. 29. 1656.

S.P. 18.124.108*

93

APPENDIX 4 THE OTHER GENERALS AT SEA

Richard Deane A former merchant shipmaster from Devon, he joined the Parliamentary army in the Civil War and became commander of the artillery in the army of the Earl of Essex and later, the New Model Army and Comptroller of Ordnance. An Independent in his religious views, he was closely associated with Cromwell and was one of the signatories of King Charles I's death warrant. Appointed General at Sea with Blake in February 1649 he proved an excellent administrator and with Blake was responsible for putting the Commonwealth navy back on a war footing in 1649. After serving briefly at sea with Blake off Ireland in the Summer and Autumn of 1649 he was seconded to administrative duties on land in preparation for the Irish expedition, and later was sent to Scotland to command the parliamentary forces there. He was recalled to naval duties after the Battle of Dungeness, and commanded alongside Blake at the Battle of Portland. He was killed in the opening salvo of the Battle of the Gabbard in June 1653 and was given a hero's burial in Westminster Abbey.

John Disbrowe (also known as Desborough) Brother-in-law of Oliver Cromwell, held a variety of senior military appointments. He was appointed General at Sea in the summer of 1653 to oversee the supply and administration of the Navy. He never served at sea.

George Monck A professional soldier, he fought in the Bishops Wars and in Ireland. He was captured by Parliamentary forces in 1643 and was imprisoned briefly. He changed sides and was commissioned into the New Model Army and fought with distinction in Ireland. Appointed General at Sea in 1651 he did not go to sea until February 1652, when he played a subsidiary role in the Battle of Portland. He commanded the English fleet in the victorious Battles of the Gabbard (June 1653) and the Texel (July 1653). He returned to military duties and became commander of the army in Scotland. It was from here that he engineered the Restoration of King Charles II in 1660. He was given the title Duke of Albemarle and was a key figure in the Restoration establishment. He saw service at sea again in the Second Anglo-Dutch War (1666).

Edward Mountagu A member of a noble family, he fought as a young man for Parliament in the Civil War, but had retired from public life at its end. He later became a protege of Cromwell and a supporter of the Protectorate. He was appointed General at Sea in January 1656 and shared command with Blake in the expedition to the Straits, 1656. Mountagu came home with the captured treasure of the Spanish Plate Fleet in September 1656. He commanded the unsuccessful expedition to the Sound in 1659. He supported the Restoration of Charles II in 1660 and was given the title Earl of Sandwich. He continued active in naval affairs and commanded in the 2nd and 3rd Anglo-Dutch Wars and was killed in the Battle of Sole Bay.

William Penn The only General at Sea to be promoted from a naval rather than an army background, he was Vice-Admiral in the Irish Sea in 1649 and commanded the squadron in the Straits 1650-51. He fought in all the major battles of the first Anglo-Dutch War and became General at Sea after the death of Deane. He is reputed to have been the inventor of the "line ahead" battle formation used in the last battles in the Anglo-Dutch War, and later to be in the standard battle formation of all European navies of the 18th Century. With Colonel Venables he was given command of "The Western Design" in 1654, an ambitious amphibious expedition to capture the island of Hispaniola (now Santa Domingo) in the heart of the Spanish American Empire. Penn returned home with only Jamaica as a prize, and a dissatisfied Cromwell had him stripped of his command and imprisoned. Although he had expressed sincere Puritan religious views, Penn became disillusioned and joinrd the royalists. He was knighted at the Restoration and played a key role in advising James Duke of York, the Lord High Admiral, on naval affairs. He served at sea again the Second Anglo-Dutch War.

Edward Popham From a landed Somerset family, he had seen naval service before the Civil War. With his brother Alexander he mobilised a regiment for Parliament in which Blake served. Blake and Popham seem to have been friends and both shared conservative Presbyterian religious views. It has been suggested that Blake was instrumental in Popham's appointment as General at Sea in February 1649. Popham commanded off the Irish coast in the spring and summer of 1649 and was with Blake blockading Rupert off the Tagus in 1650. He died of a fever in the Downs in August 1651 and was buried in Westminster Abbey.

APPENDIX 5 AN ACCOUNT OF THE BATTLE OF SANTA CRUZ

From Thomas Lurting A Fighting Seaman turned Peaceable Christian reproduced as The Narrative of Thomas Lurting formerly a Seaman under General Blake, 1832.

By his own account Thomas Lurting was pressed into the navy as a young man after service in the wars in Ireland. By 1657 he was a boatswain's mate in the *Bristol*. Towards the end of the Interregnum he became a Quaker. He continued to serve in the Navy until 1662, suffering increasing prejudice against his new-found beliefs and subsequently sailed as a merchant seaman.

His little book is a religious testimony not a diary or a work of history. The account of the Battle of Santa Cruz was a retrospective view written much later in life. His avowed purposes in writing it were to demonstrate that, though now committed to a creed of non-violence, in his former life he had been as brave as any man, and that his four-fold deliverance from harm was due to the direct intervention of the Almighty.

The account is very much from a seaman's perspective - therein lies its charm - and probably exaggerates his own and his ship's role in the victory. Nevertheless, despite all this and the passage of time before Lurting set his memories on paper, it conforms in broad details with what we know of the battle. Lurting's ship was one of the ships in Stayner's squadron, which was sent, into the bay - he refers to "going under the general's stern".

News being brought to our General Blake as we lay in Cales (Cadiz) Bay, that sixteen sail of galleons had arrived at Santa Cruz from the West Indies, we instantly went out, and in a few days got thither, and found it was as reported; and several ships went in before us to make discovery of how they lay, anchoring at some distance from the castle, which was large and had forty guns at least: there were several forts and breast-works of about eight or ten guns each. The wind blew very right on the shore, and we coming in, in a latter squadron, went under our general's stern, to know where we should be; and were answered; where we could get room. So we ran in, but could get no room to bring up our ship, so we went astern all our ships, and the smoke being somewhat abated, we found ourselves to be within half a cable's length of the vice-admiral's galleon, of about 50 guns and 300 men; and not above a cable's length from the admiral, a galleon of about 50 or 60 guns, and having also about 400 men; and within half gun-shot of a large castle of 40 guns; and within musket shot of some forts and breast-works.

And when we had brought up our ship, we were about half a cable's length from the vice-admiral, just in his wake, or in the head of him; then our captain called me to make all ready, or get to veer nearer the galleon: for I will, said he, be on board the vice-admiral. So we veered to be on board of him; and so fast as we veered towards him, he veered from us, until we came within about a musket-shot of the shore. Then the captain called me to get a hawser out of the gun-room port, and to clap a spring on the cable, which done, we veered our cable, and lay just cross the hawser, about half a musket-shot from him; then we ran all the guns we could on that side towards him, which were in number twenty eight or thirty, and all hands went to it in earnest.

At the second broadside some of our shot, as we judged, fell into his powder room, and she blew up, not one escaping, that we could perceive. Then the Spanish admiral was going to serve us, as we had served his vice-admiral; which we perceiving, plied him very close with our guns, and the third broadside all his men leaped overboard, and instantly she blew up. There was a small castle on the other side, which after the Spanish admiral was blown up, we went to work against, and in a short time made them weary of it. And as for the castle of 40 guns, we were got so far into the bay, that they could bring upon us above two or three guns; but when we went off they played upon us with their great guns, but did us no great damage.

After this was over and we had blown up the two Spanish admirals, I took the long boat to go on board a galleon, that lay on shore near to another castle, supposing that the men were not on board; but there were some, and they lay close on board, until we came within two or three ships' length of them, and then they rose up and fired several guns at us, but being so near their ship, all their shot went over us: which I call the first great deliverance. Then on our return towards our ship, they, from several castles and breast-works, fired briskly at us with great and small shot, which came very near us; notwithstanding we all got

97

safe on board our own ship; and this I call the second great deliverance.

In a little time the smoke of their guns being gone, I saw three galleons on shore,all on boards one another; one of them along the shore, and one cross her hawse, and another cross her stern, about a musket shot from our ship; and there was a castle
on one side of them, and a breast-work on the other, with about fifty or sixty men in it, as was supposed; and the galleons lay about half a cable's length from the castle, and the same distance from the breast-work, about fifty yards from the shore. Then I took the pinnace and two men with me, and was going to set them on fire; but the captain saw me, and called me back, and sent five men more with me. On our setting forward, our ship fired a gun, and in the smoke thereof we got on board the galleon, receiving no harm (the Spaniards having left them) and I instantly set one of them on fire, which burnt the other two galleons.

And when we could stay no longer, by reason of the fire, our ship's crew not being, as formerly, mindful of us, to fire some guns, that in the smoke thereof we might have retired from the galleons without discovery, the breast-work having full sight of us, discharged a volley of about fifty or sixty small shot, and killed two of our men, and shot a third in the back; and I sat close to one that was killed, between him and the shore, and close to him that was shot in the back, and received no harm; and this was the third and eminent deliverance.

And coming out of the bay, we came within three or four ships' length of the castle, that had forty guns; and they kept their guns in readiness until we came directly over against the castle: then they fired, but we were so near, that most of the shot sent over, and did us little harm, only in our rigging. And as I was on the clue of the main-tack on board, a shot cut the bolt-rope a little above my head. And this was the fourth deliverance, and all in six hours of time, never to be forgotten by me: but I desire to be thankful to God, who from these and many other dangers has delivered me.